W9-BMT-492

Best Practices in Policies and Procedures

Stephen B. Page

Best Practices in Policies and Procedures

Includes Table of Contents Examples
and Policy/Procedure URLs

Stephen Page
MBA, PMP, CSQE, CRM, CFC

Process Improvement Publishing
Westerville, Ohio USA

spage@columbus.rr.com

Copyright, 2002 by Stephen B. Page

Printed and bound in the United States of America. All rights reserved. No part of this book may be reproduced in any form or by any electronic or mechanical means including information storage and retrieval systems without permission in writing from the author, except by a reviewer, who may quote brief passages. Published by Process Improvement Publishing, Westerville, Ohio and printed by BookMasters, Inc., Mansfield, Ohio.

Address Printing and Ordering questions to:

Stephen Page
Process Improvement Publishing
PO BOX 1694
Westerville, Ohio 43086 USA
Email: spage@columbus.rr.com
VOICE MAIL: 1-614-323-3617
FAX: 1-775-458-9867

ORDERING INFORMATION

Individual Sales: This book may be ordered through the author's website (*http://www.companymanuals.com/bestpractices/index.htm*).

Orders by U.S. Trade Bookstores and Wholesalers: Please contact the author at the above mailing address for pricing and shipping terms.

Library of Congress Cataloguing in Publication Data
Page, Stephen B. (1949 -)

> Best Practices in Policies and Procedures. Includes figures, tables, and workflow diagrams, table of contents examples, and policy/procedure URLs.

> ISBN 1-929065-07-8

> Published: June 2002   Second Printing: March 2005

Although I have extensively researched all sources to assure the accuracy and completeness of the information contained in this book, I assume no responsibility for errors, inaccuracies, omissions, or other inconsistencies. Any slights against people or organizations are unintentional.

About the Author

Stephen B. Page is the author of six books, five of which focus on process improvement, business processes, policies, and procedures. Stephen holds a Masters of Business Administration (MBA) in Management from the University of California at Los Angeles (UCLA). He is certified as a project manager (PMP), software engineer (CSQE), records manager (CRM), and forms consultant (CFC).

His employment record contains an impressive list of multinational companies including Nationwide Insurance, Atos Origin, Compuware, Qwest Communications, Boeing Aircraft, Eastman Kodak, and Litton Industries. Stephen has more than 30 years of experience in researching, writing, editing, publishing, communicating, training, measuring, and improving business processes, policies, procedures, and forms. He has written more than 250 company manuals in printed and electronic formats and 6000 policies and procedures. He has designed 4000 forms and has set up manual and electronic form management systems. He has delivered policies and procedures in printed, network, web, CD-ROM, and video formats. He has first-hand experience with the application of PMBOK Standards, ISO Quality Standards, IEEE Standards, the Capability Maturity Model (CMM), Six Sigma, and the Malcolm Baldrige Award. Stephen has trained thousands of people on the principles of writing effective policies and procedures.

Stephen has written many trade journal articles. His three most recent articles are "How to Use Processes and Procedures in ISO 9000:2000 Certification" in *The Quality Management Forum* (Newsletter), Spring 2001; "Chart your Progress" in *Qualityworld* (Magazine), January 2001; and "Research: The Key to Quality Policies and Procedures" in *Quality Progress* (Journal), January 2000. Stephen is a skilled presenter, facilitator, and team leader. He has participated on hundreds of team projects. He has presented seminars on the subject of printed and electronic policies and procedures, business processes, process improvement, and forms management.

Stephen has worked in various industries, including insurance, manufacturing, telecommunications, financial banking, research and development, disaster recovery, software engineering, retail, and consulting. He has received dozens of awards for his suggestions for various quality programs. In 2001, he received the "Malcolm Baldrige Award for Quality" from Atos Origin for his passion for quality, process improvement, and high productivity.

Books by Stephen B. Page

Title	Publisher	©	URL (http://)
Best Practices in Policies and Procedures ISBN: 1929065-07-8	Process Improvement Publishing	2002	*www.companymanuals.com/ bestpractices/index.htm*
7 Steps to Better Written Policies and Procedures ISBN: 1929065-24-8	Process Improvement Publishing	2001	*www.companymanuals.com/ writingformat/index.htm*
Achieving 100% Compliance of Policies and Procedures ISBN: 1929065-49-3	Process Improvement Publishing	2000	*www.companymanuals.com/ compliance/index.htm*
Establishing a System of Policies and Procedures ISBN: 1929065-00-0	Process Improvement Publishing	1998	*www.companymanuals.com/ index.htm*
Business Policies and Procedures Handbook (Out of Print)	Prentice-Hall	1984	Replaced by *Establishing a System of Policies and Procedures*

How to Contact This Author

Stephen B. Page can be reached through the U.S. Mail, Email, Voice Mail, FAX, and websites:

Stephen B. Page
PO BOX 1694
Westerville, Ohio 43086
United States of America

Email: spage@columbus.rr.com
Voice Mail: (614) 323-3617
FAX: (775) 458-9867
URL: *http://www.companymanuals.com/bestpractices/index.htm*

Table of Contents

Introduction

This book focuses on the best practices for finding content for policies and procedures through your own efforts and from examples. You will be able to reduce your up front research and development time by knowing how to quickly identify and find content examples for policies and procedures. The phrase *best practices* has come to mean the "best ways to do tasks or efforts" according to recognized practitioners or authors. For this book, *best* comes from six sources: (1) the best methods for defining vision, strategic direction, and core processes; (2) the best methods for identifying topics for tables of contents and policies and procedures; (3) the best methods for setting up teams and executing the processes for transforming problems into policies and procedures; (4) the best methods for searching the Internet for table of contents and policy and procedure examples; (5) the best sources for finding table of contents examples and policy/procedure URLs; and (6) the best concepts and principles from my three current policy and procedure books:

- *Establishing a System of Policies and Procedures*
- *7 Steps to Better Written Policies and Procedures*
- *Achieving 100% Compliance of Policies and Procedures*

The first book focuses on setting up a system, or an environment, for the successful operation of a policy and procedure system. A proven writing format is introduced. The second book is a workbook that focuses on the writing format. This book is an extension of Chapter 4, "Writing Format," of the first book. The third book provides methods and tools for ensuring the published policies and procedures are followed, applied, measured, and improved.

This new book integrates the principles of my books and best practices from authors and practitioners by giving you step-by-step guidelines for aligning policies and procedures to the vision, strategic plan, and core processes of an organization. You will learn to:

- Understand the basics of vision statements and strategic plans.

- Identify core processes that support the vision and strategic direction of your organization.

- Identify policies and procedures that are needed to support the core processes.

- Identify methods and techniques for assuring management commitment and sponsorship.

- Build table of contents pages that can be used for the development of policies and procedures.

- Use five methods for finding content for table of contents pages and for policy and procedure documents.

- Set up cross-functional teams to define a problem statement, select alternatives, choose a solution, and transform the solution into a policy or procedure document.

- Write policies and procedures using a standard, consistent, and tested writing format.

- Write policies and procedures that align to the vision, strategic plan, and core processes of an organization.

- Use 15 table of contents examples and more than 150 URLs that point to thousands of examples of policies and procedures and related resources for finding content for policies and procedures.

- Use the Internet to research best practices for writing policies and procedures for any topic in any industry.

Knowing where to start on a problem, topic, or subject area is one of the toughest problems facing anyone who wants to find a solution to a problem. For example, when a procedures analyst is asked to write on the subject of nepotism (issue of employing two or more related employees), often a little guidance to the meaning of this word and a sample policy or procedure is a blessing. One of the goals of this book is to point you to table of contents and policy and procedure examples that could give you some clue as to the actual content of policies and procedures! This book starts to solve this problem of "finding content" by providing you sources, search techniques, and best practices for finding content and background information to guide you in the research and development of policies and procedures. This book emerged from comments of readers who requested examples for policies and procedures for specific subjects such as purchasing, accounting, personnel, or specialty manuals such as childcare or hotel management. In the past, each time readers asked me to provide content for their policies and procedures, I would reply:

I cannot give you policy and procedure examples because the actual content of your policies and procedures depends on your industry; environment; culture; and existing processes, policies, and procedures. You may become dependent on examples and not do your own research. You must identify your own processes and use analysis and problem-solving techniques to derive content for policies and procedures.

While I believe that you must do your own analysis and build an effective team to develop policies and procedures, I have found that there are a number of sources that can make the life of a procedures analyst easier because he does not have to "re-invent the wheel" every time he wants to write a new policy or procedure. Many U.S. government agencies, universities, consulting firms, and specialty organizations publish policies and procedures in accessible websites. This information can be useful because it provides examples of industry-specific tables of contents and policies and procedures to help the procedures analyst better understand a topic. This book accelerates the procedures analyst's process of identifying appropriate content to begin developing policies and procedures using best practices from various industries.

The real treasure of this book is Chapter 5, "Table of Contents Examples and Policy/Procedure URLs," because the chapter contains table of contents examples and URLs that point to real-life policies and procedures. The procedures analyst can use this information as "starting points" or "discussion points" for interviews with appropriate managers and employees who support, or have knowledge of, functional areas such as sales or marketing. These examples can be used for reference purposes when researching problems or topics that will eventually be transformed into policy or procedure documents. Without these "starting points," the procedures analyst faces the dilemma of not knowing *what* policies and procedures should go into a specific company manual or *what* information goes into specific policies and procedures.

> Complete table of contents examples and policy/procedure URLs are contained in Chapter 5. These examples and URLs highlight more than 2000 processes, policies, and procedures.

Regardless of your current job situation, knowing where to begin or what business processes or topics to explore is challenging. Whether you are new to writing policies and procedures or a professional with many years of experience, it can be a frustrating task to find a starting point. With the concepts presented in this book, you no longer have to be concerned about where to start each time you write a new or revised policy or procedure. Either the answer will be clear as to where you want to start working on policies, procedures, or company manuals, or you will know where to find that answer!

Readers should find this book beneficial for several reasons. Some will find that the examples of common policy and procedure topics are invaluable because they help to reduce the amount of up front research and development time. Others will benefit from the detailed chapters on actually building tables of contents and developing policies and procedures using a cross-functional team. Still others will benefit from the 150+ URLs that point to thousands of useful resources and policy and procedure examples. As you move from organization to organization and from job to job, this book can become your bible for helping you get started in any procedures job.

CHAPTER SUMMARIES

CHAPTER 1: *Vision and Strategic Direction.* Chapter 1 addresses the importance of the alignment of policies and procedures to the vision, strategic plan, and core processes of your organization. This alignment is critical for assuring management commitment and sponsorship. To enhance the knowledge of the procedures analyst, definitions and general guidelines are given for the vision, strategic plan, and core processes of an organization. Techniques are presented for using core processes to derive company manual titles. The company manual title is used to begin building table of contents pages.

CHAPTER 2: *Building Table of Contents Pages.* Chapter 2 addresses the first most difficult task of the procedures analyst, namely, finding the topics that form the basis for new policies and procedures. These topics become your table of contents or the listing of policy and procedure titles that are the basis of a company manual. These topics are used as "starting points" or "discussion points" for those individuals and teams selected to research and write specific policies and procedures. Five methods are presented for selecting topics that are suitable for the initial table of contents. The importance of Chapter 2 is to build a list of possible topics, policy and procedure titles, and problem statements that support the core processes identified in Chapter 1.

CHAPTER 3: *Developing Policies and Procedures.* Chapter 3 addresses the second most difficult task of the procedures analyst, namely, developing content from the topics, subject areas, problem statements, or policy and procedure titles in the table of contents. A cross-functional team is introduced as the preferred team type for the development of policies and procedures. Extensive methods and tools are included for (1) conducting team meetings to define the problem statement, diagramming alternative solutions, and selecting a single solution, and (2) starting the policy or procedure documentation process with a proven and standard writing format used by thousands of organizations worldwide.

CHAPTER 4: *Writing Policies and Procedures*. Chapter 4 addresses the process by which the selected solution identified in Chapter 3 is documented using a standard writing format. This chapter is an overview of the principles and concepts of the writing format from my current books on policies and procedures. A five-step writing process for document preparation and publication is presented as a framework by which policies and procedures are developed and written.

CHAPTER 5: *Table of Contents Examples and Policy/Procedure URLs*. This chapter contains more than 50 table of contents examples (15 complete tables of contents and over 40 table of contents URLs) and more than 150 policy/procedure URLs that represent the best practices for developing and writing policies and procedures from various industries and organizational departments. These sources, all found on the Internet, consist of topics, policy and procedure titles, problem statements, and URLs that point to examples of tables of contents, processes, policies, and procedures. Additional URLs with a "ton of information" are provided to guide the procedures analyst with the research and development phases for writing policies and procedures. Refer to *http://www.companymanuals.com/bestpractices/links.htm* for a website that contains the most current URLs of the websites referenced in this book. While this chapter should have been a part of Chapter 2, I thought that it was too lengthy to be placed early in the book and too important to be an appendix.

TERMS USED in BOOK

1. PROCEDURES ANALYST: For the purposes of this book, the person responsible for writing policies and procedures for an organization is called a *procedures analyst*. A procedures analyst in a department such as personnel or accounting is only responsible for that area.

2. HE: The traditional *he* is used because it is generally accepted in literature. However, every attempt is made to use gender-neutral terms. The term *procedures analyst* is preferred and will be used wherever possible.

3. ORGANIZATION: This term is used to denote a company, firm, or enterprise. Instead of mixing terms, I have selected to use *organization* when referring to an entire corporation or company. I use *department* for

those functional areas (for example, accounting, payroll, human resources, or sales) that make up the entire organization. There can also be departments within departments.

4. SENIOR MANAGEMENT: The term *senior management* is used to denote the management that reports directly to the President or Chief Executive Officer (CEO) of an organization. Other terms include top management or executive management.

5. CONTENT: The dictionary definition of the term *content* is "something contained." In the context of this book, content refers to (1) topics in the table of contents, (2) policies and procedures contained within a company manual, and (3) words and paragraphs that form the basis of a policy or procedure document. Put another way, content in this third point is the information, diagrams, tables, and processes of a policy or procedure, or anything placed within the body of a policy or procedure document.

6. COMPANY MANUAL: A *company manual* can be either printed, as in a physical binder, or displayed electronically, as on a network or on an Intranet or Internet website. While a company manual can be "virtual," for the purposes of this book, the term will refer to a physical binder with printed policies and procedures. I chose this usage because although the majority of organizations publish policies and procedures in a variety of formats, the physical manual is still the most prevalent format.

HOW TO USE THIS BOOK

This book contains theoretical and practical experience, with the emphasis on practical. The purpose of this book is to help you understand the importance of policies and procedures to your organization and to provide easy ways to develop content. You can apply this book in several ways:

- Start with Chapter 1 and apply the principles as you move through each chapter.

- Start with Chapter 5, study the table of contents examples, open the URLs in your browser, and study the content in the policy and procedure examples.

- Pick and choose which principles and concepts you like and add them to your skill set.

USING THE CONTENT IN CHAPTER 5

Chapter 5, "Table of Contents Examples and Policy/Procedure URLs," contains examples, 150+ URLs, and instructions that can be used to help you find the "starting points" for writing or revising policies and procedures. More than 60+ URLs reference several thousand policy and procedure examples from a variety of industries. While I believe that these examples, URLs, and actual policies and procedures will be a great time saver, these materials are not "silver bullets" and you cannot expect to use them without change. Your industry, culture, environment, management viewpoints, and current ways of doing things might be different, and your employees might have their own ideas and opinions. These materials will be helpful as you integrate them with your own set of ideas and experience. I am giving you a head start; so make good use of this book! Get started now.

ALPHABETICAL LIST OF MANUALS REFERENCED

Accounting	Administrative Policies and Procedures	Airport Policies and Procedures
Auditing	Banking	Child Care
Church	Comptroller's Office	Computer and Network Usage
Computer Security	Continuity Planning	Cost Accounting
Credit Union	Criminal Justice	Department of Public Safety
Desktop Standards	Elections	Emergency Services
E-Services	Facilities	Financial Administration
Fiscal Management	Grant Accounting	Hotel Management
Information Technology	Infrastructure	Insurance
Intercollegiate Athletes	Library Services	Medicare & Medicaid
Nursing	Patient Handbook	Payroll
PC Standards	Personnel	Power Plant Billing
Project Management	Property Control	Purchasing
Records Management	Risk Management	Social Services
Software Engineering Process Handbook	Telecommunications	Training
Travel & Business	University Governance	University Handbook
Various Manuals	Web Accessibility	

ACKNOWLEDGEMENTS

Thanks go to the readers who asked for this book. The information contained herein will answer many questions and provide insight into (1) best practices for developing and writing policies and procedures, (2) identification of content for tables of contents and policies and procedures in a variety of industries and organizational departments, and (3) Internet search techniques for locating content and reference materials for the development of new or revised policies and procedures.

Many thanks go to Mike Tarrani, an IT consultant, who specializes in process improvement and IT policies and procedures. He provided ideas that made their way into this book. Mr. Tarrani makes available a wide array of resources from his website at *http://www.tarrani.net*. Many of these resources directly or indirectly support the approach taken in this book.

I wish to thank Lisa Rosenberger for taking the time to edit this book. I believe that her editing has greatly improved its content and readability. Lisa is a technical writer in the Department of Zoology at Miami University (Oxford, Ohio). She holds an advanced degree in technical and scientific communication, with a special emphasis in the environmental sciences.

Thanks go to my wife, who has given me endless support to write yet another book.

Chapter 1

Vision and Strategic Direction

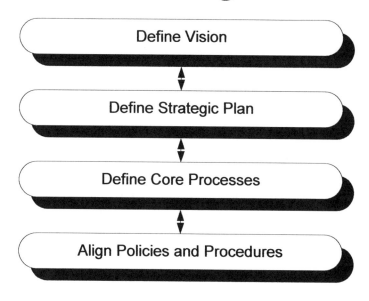

CHAPTER FOCUS

This chapter focuses on the alignment of policies and procedures with the vision, strategic plan, and core processes of an organization. Each component of this *alignment continuum* is explained to demonstrate the importance for the procedures analyst to gain a foothold in the vision creation and strategic planning processes. This alignment continuum is crucial because it can guide the procedures analyst in the important task of relating the content of policies and procedures to the vision and strategic planning processes. The procedures analyst can be assured of support for his efforts to create and maintain a system of policies and procedures when the goals and objectives of policies and procedures are evident in an organization's vision statement and strategic plan. The future of procedures analysts often rests on continual support from senior management.

As you will see, when feasible and possible, the procedures analyst should play a role in the definition and documentation of an organization's vision, strategic plan, and core processes. While this chapter provides you with the basic definitions for the four components of the alignment continuum, this chapter does not provide complete guidelines for creating a vision and a strategic plan. Refer to the books contained in this chapter and in the "References" section for several excellent books on vision creation and strategic planning.

ALIGNMENT CONTINUUM

The phrase *alignment continuum* is used to describe the relationship of the four components of the alignment continuum (vision, strategic plan, core processes, and policies and procedures). The ideal alignment is linear and starts with a vision and continues with the strategic plan, core processes, and policies and procedures. While the ideal is not always practical or possible, it still should be the organization's goal to achieve the alignment of these four components backwards and forwards. The development of these components is considered a continuous and iterative process. As each component is developed and published, you should revisit each of the other three components and determine if modifications are needed to maintain the alignment. Once the alignment continuum is established, it is important to retain the linear interactions. For example, as policies and procedures are published, the procedures analyst should assure that:

- ♦ The vision is reviewed to determine if it should be modified to reflect the current scope of the system of policies and procedures.
- ♦ The strategic plan is still doable in the published time frame.
- ♦ The core processes are revisited to determine if they should be increased or decreased in number and if they cover all aspects of the system of policies and procedures.

The components of the alignment continuum can be briefly defined as follows:

1. A *vision* captures an organization's purpose and values, and controls the destiny of an organization.

2. A *strategic plan* is a roadmap for the accomplishment of the vision. The plan defines and documents the core processes.

3. *Core processes* are the primary business processes for an organization. They are the key business drivers that support the strategic direction and drive the direction of lower-level processes, policies, and procedures.

4. *Policies and procedures* are a set of documents that establishes guidelines toward accepted business strategies and objectives; and provide instructions

10

necessary to carry out a policy statement. These policies and procedures support the core processes, and provide a framework for planning, action, and decision-making for management and employees.

The books *Vision in Action, The Mission-Driven Organization,* and *Process Innovation* are three excellent resources that address the importance of the integration of an organization's strategic goals into day-to-day management decisions (system of policies and procedures). While the primary aim of the procedures analyst is to satisfy the intent of the core processes, he can gain added management support by demonstrating direct ties from his policy and procedure documents to the vision, strategic plan, and core processes.

In some organizations, the strategic plan, core processes, or even the policies and procedures are developed in advance of the vision. For example, an organization might choose to identify the core processes before tackling the vision and strategic plan. The logic seems simple: How can you write a vision and strategic plan without knowing the primary drivers of the business? Other organizations follow the ideal goal and create the first three components (vision, strategic plan, and core processes) either in sequence or in parallel. Work can be started on the fourth component (policies and procedures) immediately following the identification of the core processes. Regardless how you develop the components of the alignment continuum, one point is clear—if procedures analysts write policies and procedures without regard for the alignment continuum, they will ultimately fail due to a lack of organizational support, management support, or customer buy-in.

VISION

A vision sits at the beginning of the alignment continuum. A vision captures an organization's purpose and values, and controls the destiny of an organization. A common vision defines the benefits a customer, employee, shareholder, or society can expect from an organization. A vision is often written as a single paragraph and is called a *vision statement*. The vision statement usually has three components (WALL):

1. *Mission statement:* A written statement of purpose, crafted to inspire employees to commit to the organization's vision. The mission statement serves as a vehicle to coordinate actions and efforts.

2. *Glossary:* List of important words and phrases in the mission statement; this prevents different interpretations of the mission.

3. *Guiding principles:* Crucial values that direct employees' relationships with customers and one another.

The authors of the book *The Mission-Driven Organization* conducted a study of vital, energetic companies and found that their success is almost always driven by the creativity, enthusiasm, and expertise of their entire work force. The three elements of such success are shared purpose, shared values, and commitment of leadership. These three elements should be reflected in every vision statement.

The development of a vision statement relies on (1) a clear understanding of organizational strengths and weaknesses and (2) knowledge of innovative activities undertaken by competitive companies and other organizations. The vision statement is in the first step in making *vision* a reality for every member of the organization. The vision creation process is important to the procedures analyst because it can define the principles and values that drive the strategic plan, a document that describes the roadmap to the future and the core processes. The core processes drive the direction of the policies and procedures of an organization.

The procedures analyst should make every effort to align the content of policies and procedures to the vision statement. For example, if a vision statement contains words or phrases such as "provide highest standards of quality" or "we outperform our competitors in meeting our customers' needs," the procedures analyst could use statements such as "standards," "quality," or "meeting a customer's needs," in the body of his policies and procedures.

STRATEGIC PLAN (Strategic Direction)

With a vision statement created, the next step is to create a strategic plan that determines where an organization is going over the next several years and how it will get there. A strategic plan can be thought of as a roadmap an organization uses to achieve the vision. A strategic plan is a comprehensive document of the organization's purpose and mission, objectives, strategy, and action plan. The successful implementation of a strategic plan should reduce operating cost; increase customer satisfaction; create a responsive, flexible, and disciplined business system; encourage interdepartmental cooperation; develop opportunities for breakthroughs; empower managers and employees to get things done; eliminate wasteful efforts on projects not in the strategic plan; avoid conflicts in plans for technology, manufacturing, and marketing; and focus resources toward achievable financial goals. The first step in converting a vision into an achievable plan is the development of four or five strategies that add to the plan. Customer loyalty and satisfaction, cost of poor quality, organizational culture and satisfaction, and core processes are the key areas to include in a strategic plan.

A strategic plan should:

1. Serve as a framework for actions and decisions and for accomplishing the intent of the vision.

2. Explain the business to others to inform, motivate, and involve them.

3. Assist benchmarking and performance monitoring efforts.

4. Stimulate change and become the building blocks for the next strategic plan.

With a sound strategic plan, the next step is to develop specific and measurable strategic goals that fall within a set time—usually one to two years. Seven areas should be considered for strategic goals: product performance, cost of poor quality, competitive performance, quality improvement, performance of business processes, customer satisfaction, and customer loyalty and retention.

Although there are good books on creating a strategic plan, I am including a reference to an excellent website, called *PlanWare*, that addresses strategic planning and provides outstanding resources for your use. This useful website includes white papers on business ideas, venture strategies, strategic planning, business plans, planning insights, financial projections, cashflow forecasts, and working capital. Templates are included for most of the white papers. Created by an Irish company, Invest-Tech Limited, *PlanWare* is located at *http://www.planware.org/strategy.htm*.

CORE PROCESSES

While the strategic plan is designed to ensure the accomplishment of a vision, one of its key components is the identification of core processes (the rest of this chapter will concentrate on the core processes and not other components of a strategic plan). Core processes support the vision and are the key business drivers of lower-level processes, policies, and procedures. The core processes are used to identify the company manual titles. Refer to Table 1-1 for examples of core processes from three organizations. When defining the core processes of an organization, the identification and quantification of these processes must be considered. These issues are addressed in the next two sections.

IDENTIFICATION OF CORE PROCESSES

Core processes can be identified in one of four ways:

1. Identify and analyze the processes, functions, and activities of an organization to determine the major departments or functional areas, for example, marketing, sales, personnel, accounting, or purchasing. The names of these major departments often suggest ideas for core processes.

2. Review and analyze organization charts that encompass the functional activities of an organization. The top-level department on each organization chart often represents a core process.

3. Use the table of contents examples from the information presented in Chapter 5, "Table of Contents Examples and Policy/Procedure URLs," and work backwards to derive core processes (move right to left in Table 1-2).

4. Use the core processes examples from Table 1-1 below as a starting point for defining your own list of core processes.

IBM	Xerox	British Telecom
Market information capture	Customer engagement	Direct business
Market selection	Inventory management and	Plan business
Requirements	logistics	Develop processes
Development of hardware	Product design and	Manage process operation
Development of software	engineering	Provide personnel support
Development of services	Product maintenance	Market products and services
Production	Technology management	Provide customer service
Customer fulfillment	Production and operations	Manage products and
Customer relationship	management	services
Service	Market management	Sell products and services
Customer feedback	Supplier management	Provide consultancy services
Marketing	Information management	Plan the network
Solution integration	Business management	Manage information
Financial analysis	Human resource	resource
Plan integration	management	Manage finance
Accounting	Leased and capital asset	Provide technical research
Human resources	management	and development
IT infrastructure	Legal	

Table 1-1: Examples of Core Processes (DAVENPORT, 1993)

QUANTIFICATION OF CORE PROCESSES

This issue of how many core processes are "right" involves the question of whether it is the quantity or quality of core processes that matters. A typical organization has 10 to 20 core processes. Others believe that there should only be three processes: developing new products, delivering products to customers, and managing customer relationships. The difficulty of selecting the "right" number of core processes is based on the assumption that processes are almost infinitely divisible; the activities involved in fulfilling a customer order, for example, can be viewed as one process or hundreds. By constricting the number of core processes, it will be easier to identify a manageable set of policies and procedures that support and put into effect desired outcomes.

The appropriate number of core processes reflects a trade-off between managing process interdependence and ensuring that process scope is manageable. Regardless how an organization defines its processes, the results are the same: *a list of core processes that becomes the guiding principles for an organization.* Whatever the number of core processes identified, the identification process is exploratory, iterative, and continuous.

IDENTIFICATION OF COMPANY MANUAL TITLES

The procedures analyst has the task of narrowing the scope of the core processes to a manageable scope. This decomposition process leads to a company manual title that typically covers a single area (for example, purchasing or accounting). With a title selected, the procedures analyst can initiate discussions with management, subject matter experts, and users to derive a draft table of contents. Using this table of contents, the procedures analyst should select the highest-ranked topics and form a cross-functional team to transform these topics into policy and procedure documents.

While you can use any method to select titles for your company manuals, I have tried to present a simple way of viewing this decision process. Table 1-2 shows you how a core process could be decomposed into several lower-level processes that eventually become the basis for a company manual title.

CORE PROCESS	FIRST-LEVEL PROCESS		SECOND-LEVEL PROCESS	COMPANY MANUAL TITLE
Sell Products	1	Sales	Sell Products	Sales Manual
	2	Marketing	Market Products	Marketing Manual
	3	Assembly	Make Products	Assembly Standards
	4	Quality	Inspect Products	Quality Control Manual
	5	Inventory	Store Products	Logistics Guidelines
	6	Shipping	Ship Products	Purchasing Policies / Procedures

Table 1-2: Determining a Company Manual Title

The decomposition stops when it does not make sense to subdivide the process further. The point at which a process becomes a title is not always clear. The size of the organization or the number of individuals who will potentially use a company manual might have an effect on the title. For example, in a large organization, the goal might be to create a company manual for each functional area, such as purchasing or sales. In this case, the result would be two company manuals: Purchasing Manual and Sales Manual. In a small organization, it might be management's decision to combine several or all processes into one or two company manuals.

USING THE TABLE

1. Select a core process.

2. Decompose the core process into supporting processes (first-level processes).

3. Decompose first-level processes into additional levels as needed, until you can derive a manageable company manual title.

INTERPRETING THE TABLE

1. FIRST COLUMN (Core Process): The core process can be written as a noun (for example, "sales") or as an action noun (for example, "sell products").

2. SECOND COLUMN (First-Level Process): The first level of processes that supports the core process. In this example, the six processes are the names of typical departments that are involved in the sale of a product.

3. THIRD COLUMN (Second-Level Process): Each second-level process could be converted into a "verb-noun" that supports the first-level process. Typically, there will be more than one second-level process.

4. FOURTH COLUMN (Company Manual Title): The company manual title is the result of the decomposition of the core process. For each second-level process, you could have one or more company manual titles. For example, the second-level process "Sell Products" could be covered in a Sales Manual, just as the second-level process "Market Products" could be covered in a Marketing Manual. However, you could also combine "Sell Products" and "Market Products" into one Sales and Marketing Manual. Keep these combination possibilities in mind when selecting titles for company manuals.

POLICIES AND PROCEDURES

Policies and procedures sit at the end of the alignment continuum and serve as the infrastructure of operations for day-to-day planning and decision-making processes. A policy is a predetermined course of action, established as a guide to accepted business strategies and objectives. A procedure is a method by which a policy can be accomplished; the procedure provides the instructions necessary to carry out a policy statement. Policies and procedures provide decision makers with limits, alternatives, and general guidelines. In a broad sense, policies and procedures are viewed as a set of documents that are aligned to a set of organizational core processes that are identified as a part of the strategic plan.

PROCEDURES ANALYST'S ROLE IN THE ALIGNMENT CONTINUUM

You should be starting to realize that policies and procedures are the "lifeblood" for an organization's vision and strategic direction because they provide the framework for action and decision-making. Policies and procedures are the media through which core processes and lower-level processes are carried out. You might also be realizing that it would be a good idea if you were involved in the identification and definition of the visioning and strategic planning processes at the organizational and departmental levels. In both cases, you are correct in your thinking. Getting involved early in the strategic planning processes for an organization can help you receive recognition from management which, in turn, will help you secure their commitment and sponsorship. With commitment, customer buy-in and user support will be easier to achieve.

Procedures analysts must be proactive in everything they do. They must get involved with all levels of management to make a difference in the development of the vision, strategic plan, and core processes. Getting involved is easier said than done and can be quite a challenge. Senior management often does not see the connection between setting the vision or establishing a strategic plan and creating the policies and procedures that enables these processes to happen. In many cases, procedures analysts have to make it known through their management that the skill set they develop while establishing a system of policies and procedures can be essential to the vision creation and strategic planning processes of an organization.

The procedures analyst can get involved when one of three situations exists:

1. THE VISION, STRATEGIC PLAN, AND CORE PROCESSES HAVE *NOT* BEEN DEFINED.

When the vision, strategic plan, and core processes of an organization have not been defined or published, writing effective policies and procedures can be challenging because both the direction of the organization and management commitment are unclear. Without support or direction, the procedures analyst must develop new or revised policies and procedures based on current management thinking and/or upon his assessment of what policies and procedures should be written. In this case, the procedures analyst can never be certain that he is concentrating on the correct problems, processes, policies, or procedures.

The procedures analyst should take this situation as an opportunity. Generally, those hired or assigned to develop and write policies and procedures should have a background that includes supervision, team building, strategic planning, thinking out of the box, process improvement, business process reengineering, writing, editing, and other types of skills that could prove useful to management in the vision creation and strategic planning processes. The procedures analyst should make it known to management that he has the necessary experience and that he is willing to help with the development, writing, and publication process for the organization's vision and strategic plan. When I worked at Datatape Incorporated, a division of Eastman Kodak, I was routinely contacted for assistance with departmental visions and strategic plans, in addition to providing advice to senior management on the vision, strategic plan, and identification of the core processes. Through this work, I developed strong working relationships with senior management and with the chief operating officer and president. These relationships helped significantly with securing management commitment and the communication of policies and procedures.

Working with the vision creation and strategic planning processes is a normal extension of the procedures analyst's job. I have worked in more than 10 organizations, and in 8 out of 10 of those organizations, I either was requested to help with the strategic plan or I was given an opportunity to provide suggestions.

There will be situations when it is not possible for a procedures analyst to participate in the vision creation and strategic planning processes. When this happens, you still should attempt to make your voice known. You have an important role, and there are a number of things you can do to become visible to management, including giving presentations, offering training classes, publishing newsletters, designing posters or brochures to advertise new programs or initiatives, volunteering to participate on process improvement committees, or serving on other teams that have the attention of senior management.

If you do not have the experience needed to help out with the vision creation and strategic planning processes, you should consider enhancing your education and training in areas such as supervision, business strategy, business process reengineering, total quality management, systems thinking, process improvement, or metrics. Refer to Chapter 14, "Looking to the Future," in my book *Achieving 100% Compliance of Policies and Procedures* for career and training references. In addition, the procedures analyst should make every effort to keep abreast of current thinking about the development, communication, and implementation of visions and strategic plans. I would suggest reading some of the books that I have listed at the end of each chapter, including those that specifically address vision, strategy, process innovation, and process improvement.

2. THE VISION AND STRATEGIC PLAN EXIST, BUT CORE PROCESSES ARE *NOT* DEFINED.

If an organization has defined a vision and strategic plan but has not documented the core processes, it suggests that the core processes were overlooked as an integral part of the strategic plan. By definition, core processes are one of the many components of a sound strategic plan. The existence of the core processes is critical because they provide guiding principles for the "next steps" for the procedures analyst. The four-block flowchart (Figure 1-1) illustrates these next steps:

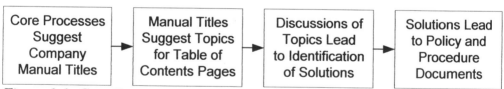

Figure 1-1: Core Processes and the "Next Steps"

The procedures analyst can turn this situation into an opportunity by offering his assistance in defining the core processes. The procedures analyst has three options: (1) contact those involved with strategic planning and suggest that the core processes be identified and documented, (2) offer assistance to work with the strategic planners to identify the core processes, or (3) perform internal benchmarking of the major functions of the organization to gain an understanding of what core processes should be defined. The procedures analyst makes an excellent choice for contributing to the content of core processes because of his involvement in the organizational functions during his normal policy and procedure activities. If the procedures analyst has responsibility for all policies and procedures in the organization, he should have a good grasp of the organization's common functions. The procedures analyst should refer to Table 1-1 for examples of core processes. Due to the importance of the core processes to the "next steps" in Figure 1-1, the procedures analyst should relay the urgency to his management that the core processes become an integral part of the organization's strategic plan!

3. THE VISION, STRATEGIC PLAN, AND CORE PROCESSES EXIST, *BUT* POLICIES AND PROCEDURES ARE NOT ALIGNED.

This third situation is most common because procedures analysts tend to overlook the importance of aligning policies and procedures with the vision, strategic plan, and core processes of an organization. The alignment of policies and procedures is critical to the success of the organization for day-to-day planning and effective decision-making. The procedures analyst can do several things to learn how to align policies and procedures to the vision, strategic plan, or core processes of the organization. First, he can study the components of the alignment continuum and understand the importance of each. With a clear understanding of the components, he can determine a plan of action for aligning the content of policies and procedures to the vision, strategic plan, or core processes. Second, he can refer to the example in Chapter 4, "Writing Policies and Procedures," that examines a "real" vision statement and demonstrates how to align key words with the "Purpose" or "Procedures" sections of a policy or procedure document.

CHECKLIST FOR UNDERSTANDING

1. The alignment of policies and procedures to the vision, strategic plan, and core processes of an organization is important to day-to-day actions and decisions of management and employees. The procedures analyst is held accountable for assuring the alignment of policies and procedures to the vision, strategic plan, and core processes.

2. The procedures analyst should make every attempt to understand the definitions and usage of the four components of the alignment continuum: vision, strategic plan, core processes, and policies and procedures. This information will prove valuable when aligning policies and procedures to the vision, strategic plan or core processes of an organization.

20

3. The title of a company manual can be derived from the core processes of an organization.

4. The future of the procedures analyst's involvement in the policies and procedures function of an organization rests on four factors: (1) continual management commitment and support, (2) involvement in the vision creation and strategic planning processes, (3) being proactive in his approach to problems and challenges, and (4) keeping updated about the latest technologies and principles in areas such as process improvement, total quality management, benchmarking, and problem-solving skills.

REFERENCES

Davenport, Thomas H., *Process Innovation*, Harvard Business School Press, Boston, Massachusetts, 1993.

Gitlow, Howard S. and Shelly J., *Total Quality Management in Action*, PTR Prentice Hall, Englewood Cliffs, New Jersey, 1994.

Hunger, David, J. and Wheelen, Thomas, L., *Strategic Management*, Addison-Wesley, Reading, Massachusetts, 1993.

Page, Stephen B., *7 Steps to Better Written Policies and Procedures*, BookMasters, Inc., Mansfield, Ohio, 2000.

Page, Stephen B., *Achieving 100% Compliance of Policies and Procedures*, BookMasters, Inc., Mansfield, Ohio, 2000.

Page, Stephen B., *Establishing a System of Policies and Procedures*, BookMasters, Inc., Mansfield, Ohio, 1998.

Primozic, Kenneth and Edward and Leben, Joe, *Strategic Choices*, McGraw-Hill, Inc., New York, New York, 1991.

Radford, K.J., *Strategic Planning*, Reston Publishing Company, Inc., a Prentice-Hall Company, Reston, Virginia 1980.

Senge, Peter, *The Dance of Change*, Doubleday, New York, New York, 1999.

Tregoe, Benjamin B., Zimmerman, John W., Smith, Ronald A., Tobia, Peter A., *Vision in Action*, Simon & Schuster Inc., New York, New York, 1989.

Wall, Bob; Sobol, Mark R.; and Solum, Robert S., *The Mission Driven Organization*, Prima Publishing, Roseville, California, 1999.

Chapter 2

Building Table of Contents Pages

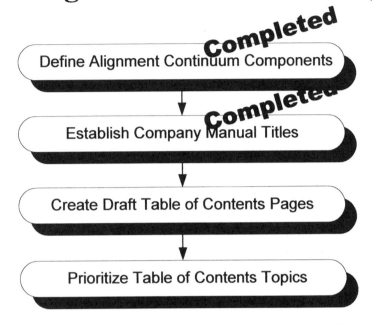

CHAPTER FOCUS

This chapter focuses on the importance of the table of contents to a company manual. With the company manual title defined, the procedures analyst can begin work on a list of topics for the table of contents. These topics are derived from five methods for building table of contents pages. The table of contents is developed, or built, in two stages: draft and final. During the draft stage, the procedures analyst identifies and prioritizes topics, subject areas, policy or procedure titles, or problem areas (hereafter collectively called *topics*) that are used as the basis for setting up a cross-functional team to develop and write policies and procedures. These topics become the "starting points" or "discussion points" for the research and development of policies and procedures. During the final stage, the procedures analyst publishes table of contents pages that contain policies and procedures that have been approved and published.

This chapter does *not* address specific details of a company manual, such as the media type (printed or electronic), the distinction between a policy and a procedure, the binder type and tabs, the electronic file structure, or the number of company manuals. The rest of this chapter focuses on building the table of contents and prioritizing the resulting list of topics.

IMPORTANCE OF
COMPANY MANUALS

The company manual is a medium by which policies and procedures are housed. The value of a company manual is measured by a reader's perception of its use. A reader wants a company manual that:

◆ Contains a complete set of approved policies and procedures written in a standard writing format
◆ Focuses on policies and procedures that are relevant to the company manual title
◆ Contains up-to-date information
◆ Represents continuous improvement efforts
◆ Contains easy-to-use table of contents pages
◆ Contains easy-to-find forms, templates, diagrams, or other documents referenced in policies or procedures

What the reader gets and expects from a company manual is dependent on the thoroughness of the procedures analyst. If the procedures analyst is proactive and has a goal to write quality policies and procedures, then he will do whatever is necessary to produce a company manual that is well received by his users. A company manual has two states of completion:

1. COMPLETE COMPANY MANUAL: All topics have been identified that satisfy specific core processes. The final table of contents has been created. The topics have been replaced by actual policy or procedure titles. Approved and published policies and procedures are housed in the company manual. The company manual is updated as policies and procedures are measured and improved.

2. INCOMPLETE COMPANY MANUAL: There are two states of incomplete manuals. First, all topics have been selected but not all topics have been replaced by actual policy or procedure titles. In this case, policies and procedures are still being researched, developed, and written. This is good practice because the procedures analyst can concentrate on the development of policies and procedures instead on the further identification of topics for

the table of contents. Second, all the topics for the table of contents have yet to be defined. Many organizations like to publish incomplete company manuals just to get something in place. As topics are added or as new or revised policies and procedures become available, the table of contents is updated and the policies and procedures will be inserted in the manual.

COMPANY MANUAL STRUCTURE

The structure of a company manual refers to the method and sequence by which documentation is laid out inside a manual. This structure should be consistent for all company manuals in an organization:

1. COVER AND TITLE PAGE: A physical company manual should have a title on the outside of the binder and a title sheet inside the manual. The title sheet could also include introductory information and approvals.

2. REVISION HISTORY PAGE: Each time a policy or procedure is added, modified, or deleted, the change should be recorded on a revision history page. This page also can be used to show improvements to the manual itself, such as when the introductory information is changed or a tab is added.

3. TABLE OF CONTENTS: The table of contents is the final list of policy or procedure titles that correspond to approved and published policy or procedure documents housed in the company manual. There are two approaches to the way the table of contents is published. First, list only those policy or procedure titles that have a corresponding approved and published policy or procedure document in the company manual. Second, list all the known topics and policy or procedure titles. Those topics that do not have a corresponding approved and published policy or procedure document could be notated with the abbreviation, "TBD" (To Be Determined) in the publication date column.

4. POLICIES AND PROCEDURES: These are the actual policy or procedure documents that have been approved and published. Each policy or procedure must correspond to a title on the table of contents.

APPROACHES TO PUBLISHING COMPANY MANUALS

A company manual can be written and published in one of two ways. First, you can write all policies and procedures in the same time frame and publish them as a group. Second, you can write policies and procedures one by one and publish them as they are approved. The first method is preferred over the second because policies and procedures can be researched, developed, written, released, communicated, trained, and maintained at the same time. More importantly, consistency and integration is more likely when all the policies and procedures are reviewed and published in the same time period. The main drawback of this method is the difficulty of training and assuring compliance of a complete set of policies and procedures. The second method of writing is a typical practice of many procedures analysts. Writing and publishing policy and procedure documents as they are completed and approved can be an acceptable practice, provided the procedures analyst is following a schedule to complete all the policies and procedures needed to satisfy the intent of relevant core processes. The advantage to this method is that the procedures analyst has more control and more time to monitor the compliance and acceptance of policies and procedures if they are published one by one.

Company manuals can be published in several media: (1) Printed text can be placed in a binder or copied to a CD-ROM; (2) Electronic text can be displayed on a network or a website; or (3) Policy and procedure information can be transformed into voice and pictures for videotape or into only voice for audiotape. Even if the company manual contains just two or three policies and procedures, the company manual should still be produced and distributed. Policies and procedures published independently of a company manual often lack a home, and compliance and communication programs are difficult to monitor and maintain. I recommend that you try to publish policies and procedures within the confines of a company manual because maintenance and control will be easier to manage. Refer to my book *Achieving 100% Compliance of Policies and Procedures* for information about assuring control and achieving compliance.

PUBLISHING POLICIES AND PROCEDURES

When the policies and procedures are published and distributed, a memorandum should be prepared that includes information about the policy or procedure document—what it is, why it is being published, and what to do with the existing policies and procedures if any of the documents being published will be replacing documents in the current company manual. The most current table of contents, revision history pages, and policies and procedures should be distributed along with this memorandum. The table of contents and revision history pages must be updated whenever any change is made to a manual. Refer to *Establishing a System of Policies and Procedures* for information on creating and publishing company manuals and table of contents pages. This same method of publication can be used to publish complete company manuals.

IMPORTANCE OF THE TABLE OF CONTENTS

The table of contents is an important document in company manuals because it provides a listing of the policy or procedure documents that satisfy the intent of relevant core processes. The table of contents can be one or more pages in length. The number of pages depends on the number of policies and procedures, the size of the manual, and the different ways the table of contents is sorted. When the table of contents is first created, it is considered a draft table of contents. When the company manual is published, the table of contents is considered final and should include the exact policy and procedure titles that correspond to the policies and procedures contained in the company manual.

The design of the table of contents is important to the way a reader navigates through a company manual. When a draft table of contents is first created, topics can be listed in any order, though, at a minimum, I would recommend an alphabetical listing of topics. Placing the topics in categories at the onset also could be helpful for grouping similar topics. For example, if you are writing personnel policies and procedures you could group your topics by primary functions like recruiting, compensation, or benefits. Researching and developing policies and procedures in groups of similar topics instead of one by one will greatly reduce the time it takes to write policies and procedures.

While you can design and publish your table of contents in any way you want, I would recommend giving your readers several ways to find information. While one table of contents might be sufficient for a manual with a small number of policies and procedures, you should consider adding table of contents pages sorted several ways as the number of policies and procedures grows. You can sort your information three ways: by functional categories, alphabetically by title, and numerically by policy or procedure number. For functional categories, think of an organization chart in a department. Categories could be structured along major functional areas. For example, if the organization chart for the human resources department has five functional areas (administration, benefits, compensation, recruiting, and safety), then each of these areas could become a category on your table of contents.

The sequence of the policies and procedures in the table of contents dictates how you set up the policies and procedures within your manual. The set of policies and procedures should be structured in the same sequence as the categories. You could also use tabs to separate the categories in a company manual. The exact location of the documents is not an issue for a company manual housed on a CD-ROM, a network, or a website because search features can be invoked to find specific policies, procedures, or related documents.

IDENTIFYING TOPICS FOR THE TABLE OF CONTENTS

There are five methods for identifying topics, subject areas, problem areas, or policy and procedure titles for a draft table of contents. While each method has pros and cons, the best method is a combination of these five. Depending on the collection method, topics might be collected in one of three forms:

- ◆ ACTUAL POLICY OR PROCEDURE TITLE, for example, "Purchase Requisition Guidelines" or "Policies and Procedures Development." When users are familiar with policies and procedures from previous places of employment, they often will give policy and procedure titles to the procedures analyst rather than a problem statement. They leave it to the procedures analyst to define the problem statement and transform it into a policy or procedure document.

- ◆ SUBJECT AREA, for example, "Payroll Department Instructions" or "Benefits Guidelines." Sometimes users just "feel" that something is wrong but they are not sure why; they just want the procedures analyst to fix it. In this case, they often give a general topic and ask the procedures analyst to do whatever is needed to produce a policy or procedure document.

- ◆ PROBLEM STATEMENT, for example, "Employees are routinely bypassing the purchasing department for the procurement of stationery items." Or, "Departments are publishing policies and procedures without going through a policy and procedure approval process." Sometimes users will be aware of specific problems. In these cases, the procedures analyst can list an abbreviated version of the problem statement in the table of contents; this version will remind him to check his notes for the full problem description. For example, the abbreviated description for the first problem could read "Procurement Problems" or "Bypass Procurement Department Problems."

The five methods for identifying topics (policy or procedure titles, subject areas, or problem statements) for the table of contents are:

1. Using Table of Contents Examples

2. Building Table of Contents Pages from Scratch

3. Seeking Best Practices

4. Networking

5. Searching the Web

While your goal is to find or define topics for table of contents pages for company manuals, your analysis will also result in background information or examples for potential policies and procedures. Separating building the table of contents pages from developing and writing policies and procedures is sometimes difficult because similar analytical techniques are often used. By considering each of these five methods below, you should be able to gather ample background information whether you are building your table of contents for discussion purposes or developing content for your individual policies and procedures.

USING TABLE OF CONTENTS EXAMPLES

I cannot stress enough, "Don't re-invent the wheel!" If someone else is kind enough to give you examples of tables of contents and, better yet, examples of policies and procedures, take advantage of this kindness and use the information to support the results of the other four methods. Table of contents examples can be a blessing when beginning research on a topic or subject area. Sometimes you will begin work on a topic, issue, or problem and have no clue where to start. I am always appreciative when fellow procedures analysts are able to give me some guidance as to the direction to take for specific policies and procedures. Chapter 5, "Table of Contents Examples and Policy/Procedure URLs," contains table of contents examples and more than 150+ URLs that point to resources that can help you do policy and procedure research and that point to thousands of policies and procedures examples that can be used for reference purposes. (This information is included in Chapter 5 because the information was too lengthy to include as a section of this chapter.)

In some instances, the table of contents examples are complete and do not need further elaboration except to assure that the topics match the type of processes expected within your industry. You may even find that some references contain more policies and procedures than you think are needed for your organization. Each table of contents example in Chapter 5 contains a list of topics for a specific function (such as personnel or purchasing). When the corresponding URL is opened in your browser, each topic is hyperlinked to a policy or procedure example. These real-life policies and procedures can give you a "starting point" as to the content of a specific topic or subject area. While these examples come from various sources, including universities, U.S. state government agencies, consulting firms, and specialty websites, content from similar sources often provides clues into the topic you are seeking and *should not* be dismissed as a possible source because you do not think it is relevant to your industry.

> Don't dismiss a policy or procedure example from an industry different from yours; it can provide valuable clues to your content or give you some ideas as to the questions you might be asking during interviews with users.

As you move from job to job and from industry to industry, you will find that many policies and procedures share common processes. For this reason, you should not rule out policy or procedure examples, regardless of its source. For example, if I am working in the telecommunications industry, an accounting policy from the manufacturing or aerospace industries will provide some clues as to the process and, more importantly, ideas as to the questions that I should be asking when performing my own research. My suggestion is that you refer to the table of contents examples as a source for your table of contents. You can use the referenced policy/procedure URLs for a source of individual policy and procedure examples. If these examples provide you the information you are seeking, the next four methods should still be used to fill in the gaps for the information collected during this first method. Even if you think you have enough information, I recommend that you still review the other methods to assure your readers that you have exhausted your possibilities when writing policies and procedures.

BUILDING TABLE OF CONTENTS PAGES FROM SCRATCH

The traditional method for building table of contents pages for company manuals has been to start from scratch, from a "blank slate," or from where nothing exists. You can use this second method for building table of contents pages in one of two ways: (1) Use this method for gathering supplemental information if the first method resulted in useful information, or (2) If the first method failed to yield valuable information, this method becomes your next choice for building table of contents pages. The starting point for this method begins with the identification of functional areas that affect the selected topic in some way. The best place to find a listing of functional areas is from organization charts. If organization charts do not exist, the human resources (or personnel) department should be able to provide you with a list of all functional areas in your organization. Once the functional areas are identified, the procedures analyst can conduct interviews with management; subject matter experts; and users who are responsible for, provide support for, or are affected by those functional areas. The procedures analyst can use existing documentation gathered from these discussions to support and reinforce what is discussed or referenced.

ORGANIZATION CHART

An organization chart is defined as a hierarchical relationship consisting of functional areas. The organization chart consists of boxes and connecting lines (Figure 2-1). The lines between the boxes represent the relationships between the people. Generally, the boxes closer to the top of the chart represent higher positions in the hierarchy. For example, an organization's president or chief executive officer normally appears at the top of the corporate organization chart, with vice presidents or other managers appearing in lower-level boxes.

Figure 2-1: Purchasing Organization Chart

Figure 2-1 illustrates an example of an organization chart for a purchasing department. For purposes of simplicity, the titles and names of the incumbents for each function have been removed. Each rectangular block represents one functional area within the purchasing department. The procedures analyst can use this organization chart to begin identifying the important processes and responsible individuals for major functional areas within the purchasing department. Knowing how a department is structured in advance of discussions should provide clues about what to ask during your interviews.

DISCUSSION WITH DEPARTMENT MANAGEMENT, SUBJECT MATTER EXPERTS, AND USERS

An organization chart serves as an excellent visual outline for discussion purposes with purchasing personnel. If you treat each rectangular block on the organization chart as a functional area, your goal is to talk to the incumbent responsible for each area. You could start with the purchasing manager and the three individuals responsible for the "Buyers," "Purchasing Administration," and "Traffic" functions. You could then ask for permission to speak to individuals in the next lower-level blocks (for example, "Shipping" or "Receiving"). When talking with this next tier of individuals, you should ask to speak with subject matter experts and with the users who actually do the work. I often try to talk to the users who do the work in a functional area before talking to management. This approach can avoid the problems that arise when managers try to tell their employees what to say when being interviewed. The questions you ask should be aimed at pinpointing the important points of a process. For example, if you are seeking information for different types of purchase requisitions, the resulting topics could be manual purchase requisitions, blanket orders, or purchase cards. The actual content of these topics is developed in Chapter 3, "Developing Policies and Procedures." Using this purchasing example, some questions you could ask include:

◆ What is your title?

◆ What are your responsibilities?

◆ Do you have people reporting to you? What are their responsibilities?

◆ What are your major process issues in this department?

◆ What are the major policies and procedures in this department?

- What would you rank as the top five problems in this department?

- What would you rank as the most urgent problem?

- What topics do you think are necessary in a purchasing company manual?

- Do you have examples of processes, policies, procedures, forms, or logs from other sources, such as previous organizations where you have worked, conferences and seminars, or peers from the purchasing industry?

- Are you a member of the National Association of Purchasing Managers (NAPM)? (If yes, ask: Can you help me out by searching for examples of table of contents from the "members-only" pages?)

- Are you a member of other associations that might provide valuable insight into what belongs in a purchasing manual?

- I have some examples of table of contents from purchasing departments (from the table of contents examples you should have already gathered). Ask: Can you review the list of topics and check off those that you think are relevant to your area of responsibility and to this purchasing department?

- Can you recommend other sources for identifying table of contents pages for the purchasing manual?

The answers to these and other questions will provide a good start for identifying topics for the table of contents for the purchasing company manual. In addition to these discussions, the procedures analyst should be requesting and receiving existing documentation that could shed light on the topics being investigated. This documentation could include job descriptions for purchasing personnel, processes, policies, procedures, reports, forms, logs, guidelines, standards, or checklists.

SEEKING BEST PRACTICES

This third method can be used to enhance information collected from either or both of the first two methods. The search for the best practices for a table of contents can be accomplished in one of four ways: (1) searching industry and accepted standards for repeatable and consistent processes, policies, or procedures; (2) searching bookstores; (3) searching the Internet for published U.S. federal and state government standards; and (4) benchmarking internal and external sources to find successful and accepted processes, policies, and procedures. Each of these four search techniques is discussed below.

SEARCHING INDUSTRY AND ACCEPTED STANDARDS

The extent to which you use industry and accepted standards will depend on your industry and the type of processes, topics, or problems for which you are seeking information. A *standard* is a published document that sets specifications and procedures designed to ensure that a material, product, method, or service meets its purpose and consistently performs to its intended use. Standards solve issues ranging from achieving product compatibility to addressing consumer safety and health concerns. Successful businesses benefit from standards by participating in the standards definition process and by using standards as strategic marketing instruments. Standards also simplify product development and reduce non-value-added cost, thereby increasing a user's ability to compare competing products. Standards are the fundamental building blocks for international trade.

While there are a number of associations that participate in setting standards, I have selected four well-known standards that apply to almost any kind of business. Refer to Chapter 5, "Table of Contents Examples and Policy/Procedure URLs," for a list of additional Standards Associations.

◆ The "ISO 9000 Series" is an international set of standards that is rapidly becoming the most important quality standard. The ISO 9000 family of international quality management standards and guidelines has earned a global reputation as the basis for establishing quality management systems. The ISO is a network of national standards institutes from 140 countries working in partnership with international organizations; governments; and industry, business, and consumer representatives. The International Organization for Standardization (ISO) chose these quality principles because they can be used to improve organizational performance and achieve success. ISO represents a source of ISO 9000 quality standards and more than 13,000 international standards for business, government, and society. Thousands of companies in over 100 countries have already adopted these standards. Why? Because the ISO 9000 family of quality standards provides a consistent set of processes and procedures that have come to be expected by customers and competitors alike. The ISO 9000 Series applies to all types of organizations; it does not matter how large they are or what they do. These standards can help products and service-oriented organizations achieve standards of quality and become recognized and respected throughout the world. These standards encompass all processes within an organization. Each standard requires that policies and procedures be documented, understood, carried out, and maintained; that responsibilities and authorities for all personnel be specified; and that monitoring quality be defined, trained, and funded. While these standards provide a direction to follow, they do not provide the wording or format for suggested policies and procedures.

ISO 9000 has been organized in a user-friendly format, with terms that are easily recognized by all business sections. The standard is used for certification/registration and contractual purposes by organizations seeking recognition of their quality management system. Refer to *http://www.iso.ch/* for details about ISO standards.

♦ The "IEEE Standards" are an international set of standards that are embodied in published documents; these documents set specifications and procedures designed to insure materials, products, methods, or resources are fit for their purposes and consistently perform the way they were intended. IEEE standards establish an authoritative "common language" that defines quality and sets technical criteria. These standards are the common denominator that organizes our technical world, ensures safety, facilities trade, adds value to products, and helps drive market development. IEEE standards and practices help to advance global prosperity by promoting the engineering process that creates, develops, integrates, shares, and applies knowledge about electrical and information technologies and sciences for the benefit of humanity and the professions. These standards are applicable to computer engineering, telecommunications, electric power, biomedical technology, and consumer electronics, among others. The IEEE website is located at *http://www.ieee.org/*.

♦ The "PMBOK" (Project Management Body of Knowledge) standards, published by the Project Management Institute (PMI) have become an international set of standards for the project management discipline. Project management involves planning, monitoring, and controlling the people, processes, and events involved with a project as it evolves from a preliminary concept to an operational implementation. Project management helps organizations meet their customers' needs by standardizing routine tasks and reducing the number of tasks that could potentially be forgotten. Project management assures that available resources are used in the most effective and efficient manner and provides senior management insight into what is happening and where things are going within their organization. If your topics have anything to do with project management, a visit to the PMI website will provide you resources for your table of contents and policies and procedures. The PMI website is located at *http://www.pmi.org/*.

♦ The "Capability Maturity Model" (CMM), published by the Software Engineering Institute (SEI) helps organizations worldwide to establish consistent and mature software processes. CMM applies specifically to organizations involved with software projects. If your topics have anything to do with software, a visit to the SEI website will provide you with resources for your table of contents pages and policies and procedures. This website also includes hundreds of articles, white papers, reports, and other documentation that could prove useful for your research. Visit the SEI's website at *http://www.sei.cmu.edu/sei-home.html* for more information.

Refer to the "References" section in this chapter and to Chapter 5, "Table of Contents Examples and Policy/Procedure URLs," for sources and additional URLs for the above standards and practices.

SEARCHING BOOKSTORES

Bookstores are often overlooked as a source of information for building table of contents pages. Locating relevant books is difficult unless you know where to look. There are three main sources of bookstores: (1) physical bookstores; (2) online bookstores, for example, Amazon.com; and (3) online association bookstores, for example, IEEE or PMI.

For physical stores, you should begin by narrowing your search to specific topics such as purchasing, personnel, software engineering, or project management. Ask customer service or inquire at the information desk about the best way to locate books pertinent to your search topics. Physical stores are often limited to what are on their shelves and what is published in Bowker's "Books in Print" electronic catalogue, located at *http://www.bowkerlink.com/*. For online bookstores, your search will be much easier than in a physical store because you should be able to enter "keywords" into a search feature on an online bookstore website. Depending on your subject, I would recommend that you use keyword combinations such as "best practices" and "(insert your subject)," or "policies and procedures" and "best practices." Try similar keywords such as "standards," "industry standards," "ISO 9000 Series," "ISO 9000:2000," "PMI," "CMM" "table of contents," or "policies and procedures." Use a thesaurus to find similar keywords. Good search engines take pride in being able to offer you many ways to find the topics you are seeking.

SEARCHING THE INTERNET FOR PUBLISHED U.S. FEDERAL AND STATE GOVERNMENT STANDARDS

Searching the Internet for general sources of table of contents and policy and procedure examples is covered in the fifth method for identifying table of contents topics. In this third search technique, the subject has been narrowed to searching the Internet for published U.S. federal and state government standards, processes, policies, and procedures. The rationale is simple: A standard, process, policy, or procedure is not normally published on a U.S. government website unless it has undergone a rigorous review process and receives the approval of a high-ranking official (for example, a governor for U.S. state standards). If the U.S. government can publish company manuals and individual policy or procedure documents on one of its websites, it makes sense to use this information as a best practice for your table of contents, company manuals, or individual policy or procedure documents.

When you search the Internet for U.S. state government standards, I would recommend the following approach: Review the state site by using the standard state URL format: *http://www.state.xx.us/* where "xx" is the two-letter abbreviation for a state. For example, Ohio is abbreviated as OH. The State of Ohio website is located at *http://www.state.oh.us/.* Once at the state website, find the search feature and enter keywords relevant to the topics being investigated. A less obvious way to find this information is to use a search engine such as Google at *http://www.google.com* or Yahoo at *http://www.yahoo.com,* and enter keywords, such as "table of contents," "state policies and procedures," "state procedures," "state standards," or a combination of "(insert state name)" and "procedures" or "standards."

BENCHMARKING INTERNAL AND EXTERNAL SOURCES

Benchmarking is a preferred method for finding information for table of contents and process, policy, or procedure examples. Benchmarking, however, can be an expensive endeavor depending on how you go about it and whether you engage in internal, external, or both forms of benchmarking. Benchmarking is not limited to just one facet of an organization's activities. Benchmarking can be applied to any organization that produces similar outputs or engages in similar business practices. Benchmarking is a never-ending discovery and learning experience that identifies and evaluates best processes and performance. The goal of this identification process is to integrate best processes and performance into an organization's present processes to increase its effectiveness, efficiency, and adaptability. Benchmarking can be used to identify new processes, policies, and procedures, or it can be used to improve existing policies and procedures. Benchmarking can become the impetus for networking.

Benchmarking is a technique used to analyze information about, and exchange knowledge with, other businesses. Benchmarking has two purposes: (1) seeking out the best practices and innovation *in an industry*, and (2) seeking out best practices *within an organization*. The primary reason to undertake benchmarking is to improve upon existing performance in an objective matter. Benchmarking identifies gaps in performance and opportunities for improvement, and it sheds new light on old methods.

While most people think of benchmarking as an external activity, it can be used within an organization as well. For example, there may be one department in your organization that has been exemplary in all aspects; this department could be used as a model for other departments. Many organizations recognize immediate gains by identifying their best internal processes and by transferring that information to other parts of their organization. Internal benchmarking involves looking within your own organization to determine whether other locations are performing similar activities and to define the best practices observed. This type of benchmarking is the easiest to conduct because there are no security and/or confidentiality problems to overcome. In almost all cases, this type of benchmarking should be undertaken first, since it is inexpensive to conduct and provides detailed data. Even better, you can frequently borrow experienced personnel from other locations to help improve your own processes. Start by analyzing the best of your internal operations. Start with your current organization and do not forget to analyze divisions or sales offices located in different locations. Many organizations have parallel operations performed at the same locations or at different locations throughout the world.

External benchmarking involves looking outside the organization at similar processes in dissimilar industries. Many business processes are generic in nature and application (for example, warehousing and hiring) and can provide meaningful insights despite being used in an unrelated industry. Benchmarking dissimilar industries enables you to discover innovative processes that are not currently used in your particular product types but that will allow your process to become the best of breed. Finding similar industries to benchmark can be difficult because a competitor usually does not want to reveal its current processes and procedures to another competitor.

GETTING STARTED WITH BENCHMARKING

If you decide that benchmarking is a tool to be used by your organization, you must thoroughly understand your own processes and procedures before venturing out to other departments or organizations. This not only will give you an excellent perspective to work from, but it also will help with your credibility when you are asked questions. When using a new tool, you should make sure that you understand it to avoid being embarrassed by it. Evaluate the elements comprising the processes, policies, and procedures being benchmarked. Identify those elements that:

- ◆ Have weaknesses within them
- ◆ Have a high potential for improvement
- ◆ Are sources of delay
- ◆ Take a large portion of the total effort
- ◆ Are the source of problems

Benchmarking is often performed as a joint activity with another business with which you share information. Because it can be difficult to find competitors that want to benchmark, try approaching organizations that operate in different business areas. Look for analogous activities in the other businesses, as this often reveals innovative ideas about how to work. Think about benchmarking businesses that have a good reputation, give thorough customer satisfaction, yield high-quality results, are recognized in a field, or show an interest in benchmarking.

HOW SHOULD YOU BENCHMARK?

There are several ways to gather information about other businesses:

- ◆ Visit them.
- ◆ Have telephone discussions with their executives, consultants, and procedures analysts.
- ◆ Contact other organizations that have performed successful benchmarking.

- ◆ Consult their website and current publications.
- ◆ Study published case studies, which often can be found in academic publications.

Whenever possible, contact the benchmarked businesses. Do not trust everything you read; some facts are intentionally omitted from published reports. You may even find that the happy ending described in a report never happened.

BENCHMARKING WEBSITES

There are some excellent benchmarking websites if you take the time to look. One excellent site is located at *http://www.benchmarking.org/*. Another good site is located at *http://www.benchmarkingreports.com/*. If any of these links is not valid when you search, go to a search engine such as Google at *http://www.google.com/* or Yahoo at *http://www.yahoo.com*, and enter the keyword "benchmarking." The first 40 results of a search are the most popular websites.

NETWORKING

Networking, or interacting with others with similar interests, is the fourth method for soliciting ideas about table of contents and policy and procedure topics from different organizations—and even from different departments within your own organization. Networking contacts come from a variety of sources, both internal and external, such as training classes, symposiums, associations, business meetings, or even conversations in the hallway or elevator. A little camaraderie can go a long way when you need someone to talk with, and that business card becomes a new source of information. In this case, you would be seeking any kind of help or reference material that the other organizations would be willing to share with you. Sometimes you can get a copy of a complete manual; other times, the contact possibly can steer you in the right direction and provide additional contacts within his organization and in local associations. Obtaining a copy of a table of contents should not be too difficult. Obtaining actual policies and procedures is more difficult because most organizations view internally produced documents as proprietary.

Associations are an excellent resource for networking. The whole purpose behind networking is to contact other people and share ideas. The more people you speak with, the better the chance that you will find someone with answers regarding a table of contents for a specific company manual. These same people can also be helpful when you develop the content of your policies and procedures.

Joining and participating in local associations involved with office administration, records, or forms also can be fruitful. A little known fact is that the records and forms management associations (*http://www.arma.org* and *http://www.bfma.org*, respectively) encompass all areas of a business; the members of these associations are likely to have similar interests—making them likely networking contacts.

Joining associations that emphasize related interests also can be advantageous. Even if you do not attend their meetings or seminars, membership alone will permit you to access restricted website areas. Within most associations, there are regions, sections, and forums that concentrate on specific areas of interest. For example, if your position lies within information technology (IT) and your job title is Quality Assurance Specialist, you could join associations that concentrate on subjects such as quality, processes, compliance, auditing, metrics, testing, software life cycle methodology, total quality management, six sigma, or the capability maturity model. Within each of these IT associations, you could find sections that are specifically relate to your areas of interest. If you were interested in metrics, you could first join the American Society for Quality (ASQ) and then join a forum devoted to metrics. Another method is to find URLs for Standards Associations in your industry. An excellent source for thousands of associations is located at *http://www.ipl.org/ref/AON/*. Refer to Chapter 5, "Table of Contents Examples and Policy/Procedure URLs," for URLs that point to 10 well-known Standards Associations. If this "associations" website is not current, go to a search engine, such as Google at *http://www.google.com* or Yahoo at *http://www.yahoo.com*, and enter the keyword "associations."

SEARCHING THE WEB

Searching the Internet for subject areas is the fifth method for building a table of contents for a company manual. The Internet is so advanced that almost everything you could ever want is there, if you know how and where to look. Many of the topics included in Chapter 5, "Table of Contents Examples and Policy/Procedure URLs" were derived from Internet searches. In addition to the URLs provided in Chapter 5, you should spend some time searching the web for information of specific interest to you. For starters, I recommend that you use at least four search engines including: Google (*http://www.google.com*), Yahoo (*http://www.yahoo.com*), Looksmart (*http://www.looksmart.com*), and Inktomi (*http://www.hotbot.com*). Be creative with your keywords. Write a focused description of your search criteria. Start with a main keyword and then add descriptive words. Write down as many ways as you can to describe the information you are trying to find. Be creative and use a thesaurus for similar keywords. Try words such as policy, policies, procedures, or standards. Try combination words such as table of contents, policies and procedures table of contents, or [insert your main keyword] and combine the search with words like table of contents or policies and procedures.

RESULTS OF BUILDING TABLE OF CONTENTS PAGES

The five methods for building table of contents pages for a company manual should result in partial or complete lists of topics, subject areas, problem statements, or policy or procedure titles that could be used to develop your policies and procedures. If you have used all five methods, there is an excellent chance you will have a comprehensive table of contents. You might get lucky and find a complete set of table of contents from one of the many table of contents examples in Chapter 5 and on the Internet. Once you are confident that you have identified an adequate number of topics, you are ready to prioritize them. With these ranked topics, you can select several and use them to form a cross-functional team to research, develop, and write policies and procedures.

PRIORITIZATION OF TABLE OF CONTENTS TOPICS

With the table of contents topics identified, the procedures analyst should begin prioritizing, or ranking, the topics. Without prioritizing, the most important topics might not be tackled first. The draft table of contents should be put together in a way that assures its acceptance as an agenda for action. Using notes and suggestions from initial discussions with management, subject matter experts, and users, the procedures analyst can prioritize and group topics that can be researched and developed in sequence or in parallel. The procedures analyst usually performs this prioritization process because management holds the procedures analyst accountable for the success of policies and procedures. The procedures analyst is responsible for the life cycle of policies and procedures.

The methods you use for prioritizing the table of contents topics can range from listening to suggestions of experienced users or subject matter experts to using a matrix, decision tree, or criteria rating form (see Figure 3-3 in Chapter 3, "Developing Policies and Procedures," for a sample criteria rating form). The results of the prioritization process can be inserted in the table of contents, or they can be maintained in a separate word processing document or spreadsheet. Regardless of the method you select for prioritizing the topics in the table of contents, the managers and users who were involved in the initial identification of the topics should be consulted to assure acceptance of the prioritized list of topics. This practice will assure future cooperation and acceptance of the policies and procedures that are eventually published.

Using this prioritized list, the procedures analyst can create a cross-functional team to research, develop, and write policies and procedures (Chapter 3, "Developing Policies and Procedures"). The cross-functional team has the responsibility for developing the actual content of the selected topics and for transforming that content into policies and procedures. With some practice using the concepts suggested in this book, the procedures analyst should find that developing content is a relatively straightforward process. The difficult part is implementing the published policies and procedures and assuring their compliance. For additional information on this subject, refer to my book *Achieving 100% Compliance of Policies and Procedures*.

CHECKLIST FOR UNDERSTANDING

1. Create a draft table of contents using the five methods (selecting from table of contents examples, building table of contents pages from scratch, seeking best practices, networking, and searching the web) presented as the best practices for identifying topics, subject areas, problem areas, or policy or procedure titles to be included in table of contents pages.

2. Start networking—it will prove helpful in your efforts to build table of contents pages and when you start developing the content of your policies and procedures.

3. Make early decisions as to the media in which company manuals will be published in your organization. This decision could affect how you research and write policies and procedures; and how you design and publish your table of contents pages.

4. Refer to my three current books on policies and procedures for details and additional examples of best practices for building, developing, writing, and publishing table of contents pages.

5. Prioritize the list of topics identified for a table of contents for a specific company manual. Consult the key people who were involved in the initial identification of the topics to assure consensus and to set the stage for future acceptance of policies and procedures.

REFERENCES

Bogan, Christoper, E., English, Michael, J., *Benchmarking for Best Practices*, McGraw-Hill, Inc., New York, New York, 1994.

Carnie Mellon University, *The Capability Maturity Model*, Addison-Wesley, Soft Engineering Institute, Reading, Massachusetts, 1999.

Gitlow, Howard S. and Shelly J., *Total Quality Management in Action*, PTR Prentice Hall, Englewood Cliffs, New Jersey, 1994.

Harrington, James H., *Business Process Improvement*, McGraw-Hill, New York, New York, 1991.

Kerzner, Harold, Ph.D., *Project Management*, John Wiley & Sons, Inc., New York, New York, 1998.

McNair, C.J., CMA and Leibfried, H.J., *Benchmarking*, Omneo, an imprint of Oliver Wight Publishing, Inc., Essex Junction, VT, 1992.

Moore, James W., *Software Engineering Standards*, IEEE Computer Society, Los Alamitos, California, 1998.

Page, Stephen B., *Achieving 100% Compliance of Policies and Procedures*, BookMasters, Inc., Mansfield, Ohio, 2000.

Page, Stephen B., *Establishing a System of Policies and Procedures*, BookMasters, Inc., Mansfield, Ohio, 1998.

Senge, Peter, *The Dance of Change*, Doubleday, New York, New York, 1999.

Spendolini, Michael J., *The Benchmarking Book*, AMACOM, New York, New York, 1992.

Watson, Gregory H., *Strategic Benchmarking*, John Wiley & Sons, Inc., New York, New York, 1993.

Chapter 3

Developing Policies and Procedures

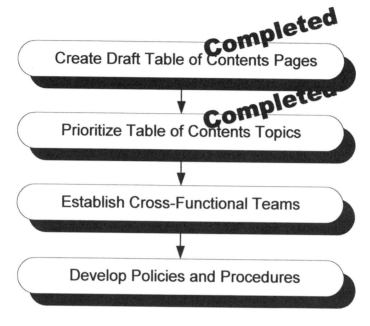

CHAPTER FOCUS

This chapter focuses on developing the content for policies and procedures. Up to this point, the procedures analyst has painstakingly developed and prioritized the table of contents topics that support specific core processes. The procedures analyst should select the highest ranked topic from the prioritized table of contents created in Chapter 2, "Building Table of Contents Pages." This topic becomes the basis for establishing a cross-functional team. The procedures analyst can develop content alone or in a team environment, though the team approach is preferred for the development of policies and procedures.

This chapter is devoted to teaching you how to set up cross-functional teams; select team members; conduct team meetings to research, develop, brainstorm, diagram, and identify alternative solutions; select a solution among alternatives; and transform content into structured policies and procedures. Refer to my current books *Establishing a System of Policies and Procedures* and *Achieving 100% Compliance of Policies and Procedures* for more information for researching, developing, and writing successful policies and procedures.

DEVELOPING CONTENT FOR POLICIES AND PROCEDURES

Developing content is the process of deciding what information goes into a policy or procedure document. This process starts from the time a topic is selected from the draft table of contents and ends when the topic has been defined, diagrammed, and transformed into a policy or procedure document. The procedures analyst should create a plan of action to set the goals and high-level tasks for transforming the selected topics into policies and procedures.

PLAN OF ACTION

The plan of action sets the goals, high-level tasks, and schedule for the development of new, or revised, policies and procedures. There is a minimum of 12 steps for a plan of action. You can add or subtract steps depending on the complexity of each topic. The choice is yours.

1. Create a schedule for the development of a policy or procedure document using a project scheduling software program such as ABT Workbench or Microsoft Project. Use a spreadsheet or word processing program as an alternative to using a project scheduling program.

2. Set up a cross-functional team and select team members for participation based on experience and relevant skills.

3. Work with the team to set goals, objectives, and success criteria and to refine the schedule.

4. Work with the topic selected by the procedures analyst to define and diagram the problem statement.

5. Identify and diagram possible alternative solutions.

6. Select one solution.

7. Refine and expand on the solution.

8. Begin gathering information to transform the content into a policy or procedure document.

9. Write the policy or procedure document and obtain approvals.

10. Publish, communicate, and provide training for the policy or procedure document.

11. Celebrate the team accomplishments.

12. Disband the cross-functional team.

The procedures analyst initiates the schedule for the cross-functional team. As the team is formed and begins its mission, the team members should be asked to help refine the schedule; this practice can help to assure buy-in from the team members.

TEAMS

A team is a group of interdependent individuals who have complementary skills and are committed to a shared, meaningful purpose and specific goals. The objective of building a team is to organize and manage a group of people so that the overall effort is productive and individual members find the experience rewarding. A team has a common, collaborative work approach and clear roles and responsibilities, and its members are held accountable for the team's performance. A team will reduce the time it takes to get things accomplished and will help to improve the organization's ability to solve complex issues by using the essential core competencies of its diverse team members. Teams give people a chance to enjoy and benefit from the interaction of joining together in solving problems.

Procedures analysts can choose to develop content alone or with a group of individuals. Both methods work, but the results might be quite different. While developing content alone might work well in a small company, working as a team is the preferred method in organizations with more than 20 employees. In the ideal team, each member performs his function in such a way that it dovetails with those of other members to enable the team to achieve its goals. By this collaboration, the whole becomes greater than the sum of its parts. When team members participate in setting goals, they are more committed to accomplishing them. The team is a collaborative group, not just people taking orders and carrying them out. A group can develop solutions collectively that the members could not have come up with individually. Teams do not exist in a vacuum; they are a part of an organization with its own vision and goals. A team helps an organization achieve its goals through the vision and the strategic plan. The team's goals and direction, therefore, must fit into the goals of the organization.

EFFECTIVE TEAMS

Effective teams display confidence and enthusiasm and seek continuously to improve their performance. The real value of a team is found when a group of minds is able to work on a problem, brainstorm ideas, wrestle with options, and, in the end, create or improve something. Effective teams do not just happen; their members have to learn and use a variety of skills to be successful. No matter how skilled you or the team members may be, there are characteristics that all teams must have to be successful according to Clay Carr, author of *Team Power*. If a team is lacking just one of the following characteristics, it will face a more difficult time than it should, and if it lacks two or three of these characteristics, the team is probably setting up for failure. These successful team characteristics include (CARR):

- ♦ Understands and is committed to clear, worthwhile group goals
- ♦ Contributes ideas and solutions
- ♦ Appreciates ideas and solutions of others
- ♦ Includes others in the decision-making process, as appropriate
- ♦ Listens to others with understanding
- ♦ Shows genuine concern for each member of the team
- ♦ Devises specific, measurable objectives
- ♦ Provides direct, prompt, and dependable feedback to team members
- ♦ Rewards the team, not just individuals

If a group is to be a team, common commitment must be a shared vision. Without commitment, the members of the group perform as individuals; with it, they become a powerful unit of collective performance. If a team is going to cooperate, members must see themselves as interdependent, that is, they must see themselves working together, building synergy. A team will not function properly if the members work alone. All members of a team must feel a sense of personal accountability for the outcome of the team's efforts. This sense of accountability is important for a team committed to defining and developing the content for policies and procedures.

TEAM BENEFITS

Developing policies and procedures in a team environment has several advantages:

1. Processes, policies, and procedures can be documented more quickly when a group of individuals is working together.

2. Customer buy-in can be achieved earlier when a group of individuals establishes synergy.

3. Personal growth can be achieved because the team environment challenges its members to use their intelligence, creativity, and skills in working on team goals and assignments. A team environment helps personal growth because it provides:

   ♦ Improved job and team skills
   ♦ Increased productivity and performance capability
   ♦ Improved morale through enhanced dignity, self-esteem, and job satisfaction
   ♦ Increased ability and desire to improve
   ♦ Better perspective of whole job
   ♦ Increased confidence and enthusiasm
   ♦ Greater appreciation of others' work
   ♦ More control over work life

4. Career growth can be enhanced because participation in team activities can give experience in leadership and team-building activities.

TEAM TYPES

There are formal and informal teams. Informal teams can be formed on an ad hoc basis to deal with many needs. Casual groupings of people come together to work on an informal basis throughout all organizations. Informal teams follow informal processes. Ideas and solutions to problems can be generated on a more casual basis and processes are less stringent. Formal teams are fundamental to an organization. With formal teams, there are rules and processes to be followed, reports to be made, progress to be noted, and results to be obtained on a regular basis. Teams can be used for a variety of purposes (PELL):

1. WORKING TEAM: Working teams make or do things. These teams do the frontline work of every organization. They manufacture goods, conduct research, design systems, sell merchandise, or keep records. They perform the tasks that are basic to the operation of the organization. Members are assigned to the teams on a permanent basis. Although there may be deadlines established for some parts, most of the work is ongoing.

2. SPECIAL PURPOSE OR PROJECT TEAMS: These teams are formed to deal with situations such as improving quality or cutting cost. They may be

created to plan a new company activity, such as introducing a new product or service. They may be appointed to investigate and report on changes in systems or compliance with a new government regulation. These teams are sometimes called *task forces* or *project groups*. All members may come from the same department or may be chosen from several departments in the organization. Members may be detached from their usual work for the duration of the project, or they may continue their regular work and function as a special purpose team on a time limit to complete the assignment.

3. CROSS-FUNCTIONAL TEAMS: Cross-functional teams are drawn from a variety of different disciplines. A cross-functional team is comprised of individuals who work in functions that "cross" departmental boundaries in an organization. This team type may function on a permanent or temporary basis. The cross-functional team is the team of choice for developing policies and procedures. These teams also are called *multifunctional* or *multidepartmental teams*.

4. SELF-DIRECTED TEAMS: Self-directed teams do not have a permanent team leader. All members share leadership. Self-directed teams have been compared to jazz combos or string quartets, musical groups that perform without a conductor.

5. MANAGEMENT TEAMS: These teams make management decisions. In some companies, a management team has replaced the job of the president. In others, the chief executive officer uses a management team to act as a "cabinet" that discusses and reaches consensus on major decisions.

CROSS-FUNCTIONAL TEAM

OVERVIEW

A cross-functional team often comes together for a specific purpose. The cross-functional team is the team type of choice for developing policies and procedures because most business processes cross the boundaries of more than one department; therefore, it makes sense to select team members from the departments affected by specific processes, policies, and procedures. The cross-functional team brings together individuals with complementary skills from various disciplines or functions and is chartered to achieve a specific mission and project goals. In many organizations, eight or more disciplines work together on cross-functional teams to develop a next-generation computer system, prepare a corporate strategy, or write policies and procedures.

A cross-functional team gets in the act from the beginning and works toward a common goal of transforming topics into published policy and procedure documents. The cross-functional team must agree on a *collaborative* approach to identify underlying issues and concerns, offer creative and innovative alternatives, work for win-win solutions, view conflict as an opportunity for team growth, help others verbalize their issues and concerns, and encourage others to work together. The cross-functional team provides an exciting opportunity for the creation of a learning community. As a team brings together people from different disciplines, the learning possibilities are almost limitless. The variety of experiences, backgrounds, and skill sets will increase the probability of creativity within the group. A broad set of skills and perspectives increases the likelihood that their output will meet multifunctional requirements.

ADVANTAGES OF EFFECTIVE TEAMS

A successful cross-functional team has many competitive advantages (PARKER):

- ♦ EARLY CUSTOMER BUY-IN: Gaining support or acceptance while developing content—not after implementation.

- ♦ SPEED: Reducing the time it takes to get things done.

- ♦ COMPLEXITY: Improving an organization's ability to solve complex problems.

- ♦ CUSTOMER FOCUS: Focusing the organization's resources on satisfying the customers' needs.

- ♦ CREATIVITY: Increasing the creative capacity of the organization by bringing together people with a variety of experiences and backgrounds.

- ♦ ORGANIZATIONAL LEARNING: Developing technical and professional skills, learning more about other disciplines, and learning how to work with people who have different team-player styles and cultural backgrounds.

- ♦ SINGLE POINT OF CONTACT: Promoting more effective teamwork by identifying one place to go for information and for decisions about a project.

BARRIERS TO TEAM SUCCESS

The cross-functional team takes hard work to succeed; success is even harder to achieve when members come from diverse and often conflicting backgrounds. The procedures analyst must keep in mind some of the following problems that impede cross-functional teams when building and managing the team (PELL):

1. Members tend to look upon themselves as representatives of their departments or disciplines, instead of as team members. When problems are discussed, their focus is, "How will this affect my department?" rather than, "What is the best solution?"

2. Members, when dealing with a problem in their special areas, often make decisions without consulting other team members. For example, a sales member of a customer relations team may make commitments to customers that cannot be fulfilled.

3. Team members tend to express themselves in their own jargon, not realizing that other members might be confused by their comments. When communication fails, team collaboration fails.

4. Some members will not share information with other members because, as they come from different disciplines, they believe they are not competent to understand it.

5. Members move too quickly to accept an early-suggested solution, rather than encouraging exploration of other solutions.

6. Members talk too much and listen too little. This is especially true of members who talk for a living, such as those individuals who work in sales, customer service, or public relations.

To overcome some of these barriers to team success, team members must first become aware of their own negative behavior patterns and take steps to learn and use different approaches to team activity. Refer to the books about teams in the "References" section of this chapter.

TEAM MEMBERSHIP

A cross-functional team devoted to developing content will have a leader and one or more team members (also called *players*, *associates*, or *participants*).

Depending on the size and intent of team meetings, additional roles might be needed, for example, facilitator, scribe, or timekeeper.

TEAM LEADER

A team leader serves the role of guiding people in a manner that commands their respect, trust, confidence, and whole-hearted cooperation. Effective team leaders have a clear vision and are able to communicate that vision to the members of the team. They develop a sense of urgency about the team's work, involve team members in goal setting and decision making, and foster a climate of openness and honesty. The successful leader also is able to understand and facilitate the human dynamics of the team and keep it focused on a goal. The most significant requirements for team leadership include (PARKER):

- Working knowledge of the technical issues being addressed by the team
- Experience and skills in managing group process issues
- Experience managing diverse groups of people with a wide variety of backgrounds, training, and interests
- Ability to work with little, no, or unclear authority
- Willingness and the relevant skills to manage outside the group
- Know-how to help the team set a mission, goals, and objectives
- Knowledge and assertiveness to obtain the needed resources for the team
- Ability to protect the team from undue and counterproductive outside interference
- Willingness to adapt as conditions change and the needs of the team evolve
- Sense of humor

The procedures analyst makes an excellent cross-functional team leader because he has most of these requirements, due to his daily involvement with processes, policies, and procedures and with employees from different departments of an organization. He is an obvious choice because management holds him accountable for the success and quality of the organization's system of policies and procedures. A good procedures analyst will have had training in areas such as leadership, team building, facilitation, meeting skills, listening and speaking skills, business process improvement tools, quality tools, metrics, vision setting, strategic planning, and supervision. The procedures analyst knows how to conduct meetings, what questions to ask, how to manage group discussions, and how to use various decision-making methods.

In many organizations, departments will want to write their own departmental policies and procedures in support of the policies and procedures published for the whole organization. The procedures analyst (responsible for organization-wide policies and procedures) is not the logical team leader for the development of departmental policies and procedures. Unfortunately, the procedures analyst often is not even aware of these departmental policies and procedures until they are published and distributed. This is unfortunate because the procedures analyst should be proactive at all times and try to be aware of any work being done on policies and procedures in the organization. While the procedures analyst might not be accountable for these lower-level policies and procedures, I do recommend that these departments invite the procedures analyst to team meetings that involve the discussion of new or revised policies and procedures. The departments might consider asking the procedures analyst to facilitate their meetings. While the true sense of the word *facilitation* is "to guide a process but not give input on the content," I see the procedures facilitator as someone who not only guides a team to complete a task, but also makes decisions. When the procedures analyst takes the leader role, he is also a facilitator and team participant. For example, I am regularly asked to sit in on these kinds of meetings. By the end of the meeting, I have often become a facilitator or have helped the leader make appropriate decisions to move the team forward.

TEAM MEMBERS AND THE SELECTION PROCESS

Teamwork starts with you and me; it begins with the individual—the team player. You cannot have effective teamwork without effective team players and, more importantly, without a diverse group of effective team players (as in a cross-functional team). Selecting the right people to join your team is a crucial decision. The procedures analyst should try to handpick the members of the cross-functional team, or at least try to be given the opportunity to set the criteria by which members are selected. The procedures analyst should:

1. Identify functional areas where the selected topic crosses departmental boundaries.

2. Contact each appropriate functional manager to discuss possible candidates for the cross-functional team. Present the purpose, objectives, and amount of involvement, responsibilities, duration, and complexity of the job to the functional manager.

3. Give selection criteria to the functional manager (see next page).

4. Interview prospective team members, if given the opportunity.

5. After a team member is selected and becomes a regular participant, report the team member's progress to the functional manager per an agreed upon schedule.

Whether the procedures analyst selects the team members, is given the opportunity to interview potential team members, or must rely on a functional manager to select qualified team members, the following selection criteria should be considered when selecting team members:

♦ Responsibility and drive for finding solutions to problems
♦ Relevant expertise
♦ Know-how to find and obtain data or technical advice
♦ Respected as a subject matter expert
♦ Compassionate and proactive self-image
♦ Authority to commit department resources
♦ Time to participate
♦ Time to follow up on assignments
♦ Ability to work in teams
♦ Credibility with other team members
♦ A desire to be a part of the team
♦ Belief that processes can be improved
♦ Willingness to embrace and lead change

The individuals selected should be experts in the departmental processes, policies, or procedures. The procedures analyst should favor those individuals with diverse backgrounds, people skills, and a willingness to help move the organization forward with streamlined policies and procedures that align with the organization's vision, strategic plan, and core processes.

The team member is expected to participate, actively listen to opinions of others, stand up for what he believes, cooperate with and support teammates, praise others for doing well, and show his appreciation for members who have been helpful.

TEAM SIZE

Bigger is not always better, especially when it comes to cross-functional teams. Researchers who study team productivity have concluded that as team membership increases, the individual productivity of team members decreases, because members are spending more of their time communicating about the task to others. According to Parker, *"Although optimal size will depend on the specific team mission, in general, optimal team size is about four to six members, with ten to twelve being the maximum for effectiveness."* Cross-functional teams seem to be prone to becoming too large to be effective.

The procedures analyst must pay attention to the size of the cross-functional team when he is asking for individuals to join the team. Team size and the development of policies and procedures are often dependent on the topics selected, size of the organization, number of resources available, and commitment from management. Two approaches for managing team size are:

1. Use a *core team* approach, whereby the procedures analyst selects representatives of the functions most critical to the achievement of the team's goals. Typical team size is from five to eight people. The core team provides leadership and makes important decisions for a project. Each member of the core team will act as a champion of the team and will help drive buy-in and implementation of published policies and procedures by educating, communicating, and mentoring departmental personnel on a routine basis.

2. Set up a core team and several *subteams*. The core team manages the process and the subteams support the core team. This format is practical when a core team is too large to be manageable and when there are too many topics for the core team to handle within specified deadlines. The core teams and subteams are responsible for communication and training programs. For example, if the cross-functional team has a goal to develop a company manual for the human resources area, it makes sense to form a core cross-functional team to coordinate the process. Subteams could be created to support the core team to study recruiting, compensation, benefits, or training. The results of each study should be presented to the core team for review and approval.

MEETINGS

The Merriam-Webster's Collegiate dictionary defines a meeting as the "act of coming together" or as "an assembly for a common purpose." A meeting is often the best place to communicate information to others when direct interaction is needed—when what you say depends on what another person says. The dynamics in a group setting can help you to think of ideas that might not have come if you were alone. Conducting well-run team meetings takes skill, experience, and good team practices. The cross-functional team uses the meeting format as a forum for its team members to meet face-to-face, solve problems, criticize or praise, make decisions, and find out what went wrong in prior meetings.

PLANNING THE FIRST MEETING

The procedures analyst should have a good understanding of the purpose and expected outcomes of a meeting before it occurs. The first meeting, sometimes called a *kick-off* meeting, sets the pace for the success of the team and the purpose for which it was formed. The procedures analyst should have a good understanding of:

- ◆ The expectations of sponsors and/or departmental managers

- ◆ Who the users are

- ◆ The background and benefits of the topic for which the team was selected

- ◆ The assumptions, issues, and constraints for possible solutions to identified problems

- ◆ The expected time it will take to define a topic, select alternative solutions, select a solution, and transform content into a policy or procedure document

- ◆ The processes, methods, and tools that a team will have at its disposal

- ◆ Existing documentation that could affect or support how the selected topics are transformed into policies and procedures

- ◆ The team's strategy and how to align it to the vision, strategic direction, and core processes of the organization

Having done your homework in advance of a meeting will be helpful because team members will be looking to you to explain the purpose and objectives for forming the cross-functional team. During the first meeting, you have an obligation to the team members to give the background for the selected topic and to provide any insight into the potential outcome of the team.

CONDUCTING THE FIRST MEETING

The purpose of the first meeting is to establish a solid foundation upon which all future meetings will be based. The first meeting is a time for introductions and a time to agree on a number of meeting processes and tools. Efforts should be made to help the participants clearly understand the purpose of the team, the expected results, and the benefits. Failure to clearly explain the purpose of a team during the kick-off meeting might result in a team that resembles a group in which members are involved but not committed to team goals. Any problem of commitment should be overcome in the first meeting.

The most important components of the first meeting include:

♦ Clarifying the meeting's purpose, outcomes, goals, and objectives

♦ Establishing the importance of the *agenda* and *minutes* documents

♦ Establishing the importance of a scribe and timekeeper

♦ Reviewing the agenda and giving participants a chance to make changes

♦ Agreeing on a plan of action

♦ Establishing ground rules

♦ Clarifying roles and responsibilities (leader, facilitator, team member, scribe, or timekeeper)

♦ Establishing decision-making methods

♦ Establishing an approach to problem solving

♦ Agreeing on meeting tools (for example, brainstorming, nominal group technique, flowchart, or quality tools)

♦ Agreeing on the use of an issues bin or parking lot to capture items not on the agenda

♦ Agreeing on methods for measuring progress, success, and when to disband the team

◆ Agreeing on meeting times and duration

For information and clarification of these subjects, refer to the "References" section at the end of this chapter. The most important meeting components are addressed below.

TEAM PURPOSE AND GOALS

The purpose of cross-functional team meetings is to brainstorm ideas and accomplish team goals. Goals answer the questions *"What are we to do? By when?"* Setting goals and working to achieve them are basic to the success of a team. Team goals should not be confused with the vision of the organization. Vision is a broad statement of purpose and direction. Team goals are specific, short-range targets. The team members should set long-term goals to carry out its mission and short-term goals for specific tasks. Team goals must be congruent with those of the department the team is part of, as well as with those of the organization. Team members should be involved in setting team goals because the interaction of the group increases the quantity and quality of team ideas and suggestions. Team members are involved because:

◆ Members have a clear sense of what is expected.
◆ Each member has an opportunity for personal learning and growth when permitted to participate in goal-setting exercises.
◆ When team members participate in setting team goals, they are more likely to work hard to achieve them.
◆ Collaboration reinforces the importance of team members' supporting each other in implementing goals.
◆ When team members know what performance results are expected by every other member, they can measure progress and take the initiative to correct deviations in a timely manner.

The goals of a cross-functional team include:

◆ Defining the problem statement for the selected topic being addressed
◆ Developing a work flow and diagramming the problem statement
◆ Examining and diagramming all reasonable alternative solutions
◆ Reaching a decision on one alternative solution
◆ Refining the diagram of the selected solution
◆ Transforming the content into a standard writing format for the policy or procedure

- ◆ Reviewing and approving the policy or procedure
- ◆ Publishing, communicating, and training the policy or procedure

GROUND RULES

Ground rules explicitly spell out behavior and processes that people normally consider fair but sometimes abandon in the dynamic interaction of a group. Ground rules help to cultivate the basic ingredients needed for a successful meeting. Establishing ground rules provides a sanctioned opportunity to discuss what constitutes "good behavior," which may help a contentious group let go of some other behavior that has been getting in its way. Generally, ground rules should include how decisions will be made, what basic work methods will be used, how issues and concerns will be handled, and how to resolve differences.

Ground rules should also spell out the use of a scribe and a timekeeper for each meeting. A scribe takes the minutes of the meeting; a timekeeper informs speakers when the time is up for an item on the agenda. These two positions should be rotated; they should be assigned at the beginning of each meeting.

Examples of ground rules include:

- ◆ Encouraging everyone to participate
- ◆ Expressing all views and opinions, whether "right" or "wrong"
- ◆ Letting others speak without interruption and with respect
- ◆ Staying on the subject
- ◆ Looking for strengths, not weaknesses, in others
- ◆ Avoiding causing emotional injury or hurt
- ◆ Accepting all as equal
- ◆ Listening to other's opinions
- ◆ Avoiding side conversations
- ◆ Debating ideas, not individuals
- ◆ Avoiding early evaluation without discussions
- ◆ Being constructive
- ◆ Sharing the floor
- ◆ Saying "yes" or "no" without feeling guilty
- ◆ Changing his or her mind
- ◆ Beginning and ending on time
- ◆ Accepting the role of a scribe or timekeeper

Ground rules are normally set the first time a team meets. The time spent establishing ground rules usually pays off by keeping the group on track and maintaining good relations. In later meetings, the ground rules can be included as a part of the minutes. If new participants join, it is good practice to either review the ground rules at the start of the meeting or to speak with newcomers prior to the meeting, so time is not taken away from meetings.

ESTABLISHING DECISION-MAKING METHODS

Nothing demonstrates the value of a team as much as the decision-making process. A decision is "the act or process of deciding" or "a determination arrived at after consideration." The goals of a team decision-making process are to (1) increase the number of alternatives explored, (2) build more objectivity into the decision-making process, and (3) achieve consensus while valuing individual contributors. Managing agreement is a major component of a mature team. Members learn to test for agreement often and to write down points of agreement as they occur. Team members must go beyond simply understanding one another and reaching a decision everyone can live with to learning how to suspend their own views, loosen their grip on certainty, and emerge as a single entity. A decision that reflects the experience, skills, opinions, and commitment of all team members is always stronger than a decision made by one person, even if that person makes what is at first believed to be a quicker, better decision. Decision making can be successful if team members have the:

- ◆ Ability to be open-minded and to explore a topic
- ◆ Willingness to listen carefully to others' points of view
- ◆ Ability to find a middle ground or alternatives that can be supported by all team members
- ◆ Ability to have empathy for others
- ◆ Ability to think more in questions than in statements
- ◆ Use of problem-solving tools to aid decision making
- ◆ Ability to gain support from significant outsiders

There are two primary ways to make decisions: consensus or voting. *Consensus* is defined as "a judgment arrived at by a group or an agreement by all participants." The group should decide if agreement means "total agreement with no questions" or "partial agreement with some questions." Consensus results after the team expresses the problem and compromises are made. Consensus does not mean unanimous agreement. Everyone may not agree on every detail, but members do believe the decision to be a sound one that they are willing to support. The team members believe that their major concerns are addressed and are willing to move forward. Many groups choose consensus as their decision-making method because when everyone reaches consensus, everyone buys in to the decision. The main benefits of consensus decision-making are that everyone involved is able to express his point of view and that the decision most likely will be the best one possible. Also, since the decision is a mutual one, its implementation is likely to be supported by the entire team. Experiments in group process have shown that, in most circumstances, the analytical power of a group of individuals is greater than that of any of its single members. For that reason, the group's consensus judgments are likely to be more accurate that the judgments of an individual member.

Yet when people sit around a table and analyze a problem, rare is the team member who believes that the other members collectively know more about the problem, understand it better, and can come up with a better solution than he can, particularly when that member's opinion is at odds with the team. Therefore, the risk of consensus decision-making is that it lacks speed. If no one can leave the room until a consensus is reached, any person can stop the action. For this reason, the group should agree on what consensus means before selecting consensus as the decision-making method.

Voting is the second decision-making method. Voting is the classic democratic approach, in which the majority rules. Voting is defined as "expressing one's view in response to a poll" or "to cause to cast for or against a proposal." Voting is quick and it gives a decisive result. A disadvantage is when the results leave "winners" and "losers," and losers may not support the decision with as much enthusiasm as the winners. When a group chooses voting as its decision-making method, the team must be clear as to how many votes become a majority:

◆ SIMPLE MAJORITY: The decision is made by choosing a solution that is acceptable to more than half of the entire group, with each person having equal power (one person, one vote).

◆ SUPER MAJORITY: The decision is made by choosing a solution that is acceptable to more than two-thirds or three-fourths of the entire group, with each person having equal power (one person, one vote).

The procedures analyst may be thinking, "Can a cross-functional team that focuses on the development of policies and procedures make all its own decisions, or does the team have to involve other approvals?" This question cannot be answered easily. Any decision about how to conduct a team meeting, how to brainstorm, how to select and diagram a solution, or how to write a policy or procedure document will normally fall on the shoulders of the cross-functional team. There are also a number of decisions that might come up during team meetings that should be made by senior management or as a joint decision. There are two categories of decisions: senior management decisions and team decisions. There could be a third category for a joint decision between senior management and the team, but since senior management usually has the final say, I did not include it as a category.

SENIOR MANAGEMENT DECISIONS

- Decisions that entail the expenditure of more than certain amounts of money
- Process changes that require capital expenditures
- Decisions that change organization-wide policies or goals
- Decisions that affect customers (for example, price changes or changes from specifications)
- Decisions to change from one supplier of a key product or service to another
- Decisions to stop serving a customer
- Decisions that require bringing in outside resources
- Personnel decisions
- Approvals of policies and procedures

TEAM DECISIONS

- Decisions that affect the entire team within the limits of its authority
- Setting team goals
- Developing and writing policies and procedures
- Identification of alternative solutions
- Selection of a single solution
- Transformation of content into policies and procedures
- Designing new or revising existing forms and other documents
- Designing content for communication and training programs
- Money decisions within a budget limit

Before the close of the first meeting, the team should agree on which decision-making method it will use. Once a decision is made, every team member whose work is affected by it needs to be informed about it. The team also needs to decide what to do if it deadlocks and is unable to reach a decision. The team can negotiate further or invoke a secondary decision rule, such as having the team leader make the choice or delegating a single individual the authority to resolve an issue or to settle a disagreement.

MEETING TOOLS

Several documents and tools can be used for the coordination and execution of a meeting. An *agenda* is used to keep a meeting on track. An *issues bin* is used to record those items that team members wish to speak about, that are not on the agenda. A *minutes* document is used to record discussions that take place during a meeting. *Quality tools* are used to help with problem-solving efforts.

AGENDA

A key to the success of any meeting is an agenda, or a list of things to be accomplished at a meeting. An agenda is used to inform attendees of the planned discussion topics, activities, time frames, order of presentation, and meeting roles. If new concepts or technical or complex material will be introduced, participants should be given written information (included with agenda) before the meeting so they can study it and be prepared to discuss it. One of the most common reasons for meeting failure is the inclusion of nonrelevant subjects in an agenda. If the meeting objective is to discuss cutting cost in a procedure, do not include an item on the organization's forthcoming picnic. The agenda topics should be arranged in such a way to get the team members involved early by having something for them to do right away. Effective meeting leaders carefully prepare the agenda and control the meeting with it. The procedures analyst should prepare and distribute the agenda at least 48 hours in advance of each meeting, with instruction as to what to read and/or review. The agenda should be available during each meeting. At the beginning of a meeting, the procedures analyst should review the agenda for the team members and expand on what will be covered in each topic. This is an excellent time to ask if the agenda items or objectives meet the team's needs and expectations.

An agenda normally includes the following items:

- ◆ Organization or departmental identification (for example, department name or logo)
- ◆ Title of meeting
- ◆ Name of person who called the meeting
- ◆ Names of invited attendees
- ◆ Date, starting time, and place of meeting
- ◆ Ending time
- ◆ List of topics to be presented or discussed and estimated times
- ◆ Action items from previous meetings

- Background materials
- List of what to bring to the meeting
- Role assignments, including the name and expected roles, for example, team leader, facilitator, scribe, and timekeeper

ISSUES BIN OR PARKING LOT

The *issues bin* or *parking lot* is a meeting tool that provides a place to write ideas that are not the subject of the agenda. As a meeting progresses, any subject or issue raised that does not match an agenda item should be listed in the issues bin. While this information can be captured on a notepad, it is preferable to use a whiteboard or flip chart so the issues are in clear view of those in the room. This tool helps a team stay focused. At the end of a meeting, the team leader should review the items in the issues bin and make a disposition of them. The items could be resolved, deleted, added to the next agenda, or assigned to someone for research and follow-up.

QUALITY TOOLS

Quality tools are methods and techniques used for planning, analysis, and interpretation during a meeting; they could include brainstorming, affinity charts, nominal group technique, interviewing techniques, streamlining tools, process maps, workflow diagrams, flowcharts, or criteria rating forms. Where possible, the team should select familiar tools. The team leader should be alert to which team members need tool training. Refer to Richard Y. Chang's books, *Continuous Improvement Tools – Volumes 1 and 2,* for definitions and examples of 14 quality tools. These books are an excellent resource. His books offer simple step-by-step instructions, along with real-life examples, for learning how to use quality tools. Also, refer to Chapter 9, "Using Continuous Improvement Tools to Measure Compliance," in my book *Achieving 100% Compliance of Policies and Procedures* for an explanation of these quality tools and how to use them. This latter book uses a case study to illustrate the use of five quality tools.

MINUTES

Minutes provide an important record of what has transpired during a meeting, and they often serve as reminders to action items or assignments made at the close of a meeting. At the start of the meeting, the procedures analyst should appoint a scribe to listen to the conversations and take notes. The team leader should make the decision as to the detail required for the meeting. After the meeting, the scribe should transform his notes into a formal *minutes* document.

Copies of the minutes should be distributed to all attendees and to others in the organization that may be affected by what has transpired, no later than 48 hours after the meeting has been adjourned.

CLOSING THE FIRST MEETING

Just as a meeting needs clarity in the beginning, it needs clarity at the end. Participants need to leave a meeting with a clear, common understanding of what has been accomplished, what has been agreed upon, what needs to happen next, and who is assigned to do what and when. Toward the end of the meeting, the team leader should review actions and assignments, review the issues bin for open action items, ask for suggestions for the next meeting, set the time for the next meeting, and ask each participant if he can attend the next meeting. Meetings should be closed with a positive message, such as a summary of the meeting, some inspirational comments, or a call to action—asking members to take specific steps. Some suggestions for positive closings include:

♦ Summarizing the important points and the accomplishments of the meeting

♦ Challenging the team members to take specific actions based on the events of the meeting

♦ Making a final motivating statement to inspire the team members to take the actions that resulted from the meeting

As the team members are leaving the meeting place, the team leader should ask that they complete their assignments on time and come prepared for the next meeting. Indicate that the minutes will be circulated within 48 hours.

SUBSEQUENT MEETINGS – DOING THE WORK

With introductions and meeting basics out of the way, the cross-functional team can begin reviewing the topic or topics selected for review by the procedures analyst. Problem-solving skills are introduced that will help the team members with the conversion process from an initial idea to a published policy or procedure document. Each subsequent meeting should focus on expanding, demonstrating, and clarifying information. The six-step flow diagram below illustrates a problem-solving technique that will be used in the remainder of this chapter to transform the content developed by the team members into a policy or procedure document.

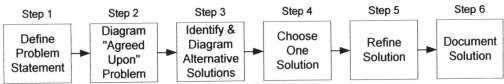

Figure 3-1: Problem-Solving Process Flow

Steps 1-5 are addressed in this chapter, while Step 6 is addressed in Chapter 4, "Writing Policies and Procedures." Topics selected by the procedures analyst from the draft table of contents become the input to this problem-solving process flow. A published policy or procedure document is the output of the process flow.

Several of the steps overlap and use similar techniques. For example, the problem statement might be diagrammed in Step 1 and/or in Step 2. Depending on the decisions reached by the cross-functional team, a high-level flowchart might be created in Step 1 with a detailed flowchart being created in Step 2. Or the flowchart might be initiated in Step 2 or Step 3. Once the solution is selected in Step 4, the flowchart might be revisited in Step 5.

STEP 1: DEFINE PROBLEM STATEMENT

The first step is always the most difficult. In this step, the team must agree on the problem statement and expected outcomes. Careful and thoughtful analysis and consensus of the problem statement up front should lead to fewer differences in subsequent meetings. The procedures analyst should explain the problem to the team and invite feedback. Frequently, problem statements start out far bigger than the actual problem. In addition, solutions are often not substantive enough to completely solve the problem. The problem statement needs to be simple and specific so that time and resources are adequate to provide the needed analysis toward creating an effective solution.

When a problem statement is already known, the procedures analyst can explain the background of the problem to the team, ask for feedback, and possibly ask that a vote be taken to decide if the team members think that the original problem statement is satisfactory. The danger of this early analysis is that the team may be overlooking the root cause of the problem. If the team votes "yes" to the problem statement as it stands, the procedures analyst should request a sanity check to validate, or double-check, that the problem statement is truly representative of the root cause. Root-cause analysis can uncover the real culprit that created a problem or opportunity, and it suggests an investigation of such issues as technology (system malfunction), people (without drive), process (poorly implemented processes), environment (poor working conditions), training (lack of timely training), and organization (lack of project structure and communication).

Problems and opportunities define a gap between current reality and a desired state. When a problem is solved, the gap closes. Often, the initial problem statement tends to cover vast territory and complexity with a few words. Before a person heads out to do fact-finding to substantiate a problem, one important question should be asked: "Why?" "Why should we solve this problem at all?" Or, more specifically, "What are the business objectives at risk?" Risks could include loss of revenue, increasing cost, diminished customer service, noncompliance with regulations, and loss of competitive advantage. Without risk, there is little justification for solving a problem. Just as important, the business risks "hook" the attention of team members during the process.

Through open discussions and compromises, a problem statement can be described clearly. If the team cannot agree on a problem statement in a reasonable amount of time, two additional techniques could be used to further explain the problem: restating and flowcharting the problem statement.

RESTATING THE PROBLEM STATEMENT

The initial problem statement is not always correct. The team cannot take for granted everything the procedures analyst says or suggests. How many times have you discovered, halfway through a problem's solution, that the initial problem statement was far off the mark? I have seen numerous examples of people whose narrow definition of a problem caused an analysis to be shortsighted, overlooking alternative—and possibly more beneficial—solutions. There are four common pitfalls to defining a problem that can be avoided through thorough definition, restatement, and paraphrasing (JONES):

1. No focus—definition is too vague or broad.

2. Misdirected focus—definition is too narrow.

3. Problem statement is assumption-driven.

4. Problem statement is solution-driven.

Morgan D. Jones, author of *The Thinker's Toolkit*, recommends an indirect approach: *"restate (redefine) the problem in as many different ways as we can think of."* Jones continues, *"The aim of problem restatement is to broaden our perspective of a problem, helping us to identify the central issues and alternative solutions and increasing the chance that the outcome our analysis produces will fully, not partially, resolve the problem."* The cross-functional team must make every effort to re-evaluate its thought processes and decide if the problem statement is the best for the moment. Every problem can be viewed from multiple conflicting perspectives. Biases and mind-sets determine our perspective of problems. This perspective drives our analysis, our conclusions, and, ultimately, our recommendations.

There are countless ways to creatively restate problems. The following five techniques are effective (JONES):

1. PARAPHRASE: Restate the problem using different words without losing the original meaning.

2. 180 DEGREES: Turn the problem on its head.

3. BROADEN THE FOCUS: Restate the problem in a larger context.

4. REDIRECT THE FOCUS: Boldly, consciously change the focus.

5. ASK "WHY": Ask "why" of the initial problem statement. Then formulate a problem statement based on the answer. Ask "why" again and restate the problem based on the answer. Repeat this process at least five times, until the essence of the real problem emerges.

FLOWCHARTING THE PROBLEM STATEMENT

The use of a flowchart is an excellent way to visually view a problem statement through the use of simple symbols, lines, or words to display the activities and sequence of a process. The flowchart tool can be used anytime diagramming is needed. The primary objective of a flowchart is to break down the problem into component parts and to examine how they go together. The goal is to understand the problem, not describe it, although the more you understand the problem, the more accurately you can define it. Flowcharting is an invaluable tool for understanding the inner workings of and relationships between business processes. Differences between the ways the activity is supposed to be conducted and the way it is actually conducted will emerge.

Visually illustrating a problem statement in a block-diagram flowchart will help the team view a problem from a different perspective. A *block diagram* is the simplest and most prevalent type of flowchart as it provides a quick, uncomplicated view of the process. A high-level block diagram is used to develop a preliminary understanding of the process and its boundaries for Step 1. A detailed diagram can be used when diagramming the current situation (Step 2), the alternative solutions (Step 3), and when refining the selected solution (Step 5). This high-level flowchart should be used to identify what is included in the process, the inputs, the outputs, and the departments involved.

Using this graphical representation and the information gathered from discussions with users, the procedures analyst should ask that a consensus be reached on the problem definition and on the expected outcomes before moving to the next step.

STEP 2: DIAGRAM "AGREED UPON" PROBLEM

The team starts this step by gathering information from brainstorming techniques, interviews, questionnaires, or surveys. Coupled with the high-level diagram created in Step 1, this information is used to diagram the current situation and to diagram the alternative solutions. The goal of this step is to develop a detailed and comprehensive diagram for the "agreed upon" problem statement defined in Step 1. Diagrams can communicate types of information among the team members more efficiently than text, and they can help bridge language and vocabulary barriers among different team members. Graphical documentation and/or process diagramming tools are useful for (1) arriving at and documenting a common understanding of current processes and (2) diagramming how an organization performs its essential business activities. These diagrams include detailed information about how each activity is triggered, what resources are used to accomplish the activity, and what deliverables are created by the activity. The combination of textual and graphical representations can paint a full picture of the intended system and can help detect inconsistencies, ambiguities, errors, or omissions.

GENERATION OF IDEAS

The methods by which ideas are generated can be used anywhere, anytime by a cross-functional team to identify the current environment and to generate new ideas and improvements. The procedures analyst and the team members can conduct brainstorming sessions, one-on-one interviews, telephone calls, or send out questionnaires and surveys to obtain information for a problem or process. These sources can be used to (1) generate ideas from within the group by asking questions and brainstorming; (2) solicit information from individuals or groups outside of the cross-functional team; and (3) research existing documentation for processes, policies, procedures, or forms. Use these sources and then add your own sources as needed.

When starting a new flowchart or elaborating on a current one, the following kinds of questions should help you diagram the current situation or problem:

- What is the problem and what is it not?
- What do you like about the current situation and want to save?
- Where does the process start and end?
- What are the boundaries of the problem?
- What are the interfaces?
- What is the current technology?
- What are the strengths and weaknesses of the problem?
- What would you like to change?
- Who owns the problem?
- What opportunities are out there?

Brainstorming Ideas

The team should explore brainstorming as a primary means of soliciting ideas from one another within the group environment. Brainstorming is used to identify problems, potential solutions, or courses of action. The term *brainstorming* is a group facilitation technique or practice that encourages participation from all group members, whatever their roles and relationships within the organization. The purpose of brainstorming is to generate creative ideas about a topic and to allow ideas of every kind to flourish, randomly and spontaneously, and multiply, thereby enriching the thinking process and the inventiveness of solutions. Team members can blurt out ideas in any order, and all ideas should be fair game.

A typical brainstorming session should last a short amount of time, say 15 minutes. In response to a question, team members are permitted to say whatever they feel is important anytime they want. Through this brainstorming activity, team members can identify important issues, concerns, or problems; create a list of causes; and generate possible solutions or answers. One disadvantage of brainstorming is that there is no guarantee that everyone will have an opportunity to make a suggestion. To account for this disadvantage, there are many rules for brainstorming:

- Start out by clearly stating the objective of the brainstorming session.
- Generate as many ideas as possible.

- Let your imagination soar.
- Quantity, not quality, is encouraged.
- Anything goes, all ideas are valid.
- Adding to ideas of others is encouraged.
- No discussion of issues is allowed (do this later).
- Everyone participates, no observers.
- One person speaks at a time.

Information gathering is an informal process. As ideas come in, the team leader or facilitator can write them on sticky notes and post the notes on easel charts or on the wall. The information is then *pruned*, meaning that similar ideas are combined and outrageous ideas are eliminated. Brainstorming sessions usually produce a number of ideas that can then be evaluated in terms of their relative benefits, costs, risks, and time frames. If this brainstorming technique is not adequate, there are several variations to brainstorming that you could use:

1. REVERSE BRAINSTORMING: List all the things that do not work with a process, system, or product (HARRINGTON-MACKIN).

2. FORCED RELATIONSHIPS: Isolate the parts of a problem; analyze the various relationships of the parts; look for patterns; and develop ideas based on the patterns (HARRINGTON-MACKIN).

3. SLIP METHOD: After freewheeling and round robin brainstorming, ask people to put a last great idea on a slip of paper. Without fail, the slip method yields at least one or two more ideas (HARRINGTON-MACKIN).

4. NOMINAL GROUP TECHNIQUE: Ask questions and get answers from team members one at a time. This is a structured brainstorming technique that permits team members time to silently think about ideas before being asked to present them. When the team leader or facilitator asks a member to present an idea, he can add to the previous ideas or present new ideas that may have been stimulated by the discussion. One advantage of this brainstorming variation is that every member of the team is given an equal opportunity to make suggestions. The nominal group technique encourages individual team members to:

- Generate ideas that address a question or issue without undue influence from others
- Present the ideas independently
- Participate when the ideas are discussed and voted on as a group

Fact-finding Outside the Team Environment

During team meetings, there will be occasions to invite employees with knowledge on specific subjects to participate in the discussions. At times, this practice will not prove timely, and it will be necessary for team members to meet with users outside of the team environment. Before initiating fact-finding, the team should agree on what information is needed, how it will be gathered, and who is responsible. Options for gathering this information include:

♦ Discussions with management, subject matter experts, and users
♦ Interviews in person or by telephone
♦ Video conferencing or teleconferencing
♦ Surveys
♦ Questionnaires
♦ Focus meetings
♦ Benchmarking
♦ Networking
♦ Analysis of existing printed and electronic documents, including business processes, policies, or procedures; standards; forms; regulations; or other documentation

DIAGRAMMING GUIDELINES

Whether you diagram first and then generate ideas to fill in the gaps in a process or flowchart; or you generate ideas first and then diagram the process, the result is the same: a visual representation of the current situation or problem. If you created a high-level block diagram as suggested in Step 1, you might want to start generating ideas before expanding the diagram. Whether you generate ideas or diagram first does not make any real difference as long as you do them both. Diagramming principles and methods for diagramming the current situation will be addressed below. These principles can be applied to Steps 1-5.

Diagramming Principles

Diagramming principles focus on how to subdivide a problem and on methods and techniques for illustrating a process as a picture (for example, a flowchart or a process map). While there are several good books written on diagramming techniques, I have found that David Straker's *Rapid Problem Solving with Post-It® Notes* is an excellent book that every procedures analyst should read. The use of Post-It® Notes for problem-solving exercises in meetings is a familiar method to many facilitators and team leaders. Straker's principles are especially useful when diagramming a problem. He contends that problems are almost always made up of individual pieces of information that are related to each other in some way. The size of the problem is simply determined by the number of information pieces and the number and type of relationships *among* these pieces. He states, *"Whether your problem is to build a house, analyze competitive strategy, or plan a meal, all you need to know is what the pieces are and how they may be organized to help you understand the problem and produce an effective solution."* Straker addresses "chunking" and "problem patterns" as methods for subdividing a problem statement.

1. CHUNKING: Your mind works by processing information one individual piece, or *chunk*, at a time. The chunk may be simple, like "a brick," or more complex, such as "a house." Information about problems also comes in chunks and often can be written in short phrases or sentences. These chunks can be captured using *sticky notes* or some kind of flowcharting technique. You can solve problems by finding all the chunks, arranging them into meaningful patterns, and focusing on the important parts.

2. PROBLEM PATTERNS: There are two ways to arrange chunks:

   ♦ *Lists.* Simple collections of chunks that are ordered or nonordered. The simplest way to group information chunks is to list them, one after the other. An ordered list is a list sorted in order of importance. An example of a list is a prioritized table of contents.

   ♦ *Trees. S*imple hierarchical "parent-and-child" relationships that can be built top-down or bottom-up. Chunking works in both directions. Given a piece of information, you can "chunk down" by breaking it into its constituent parts or "chunk up" by finding what it is a part of. Connecting these different levels of chunks forms a tree-shaped structure. An example of a "tree" is an organization chart. A complex tree structure is sometimes called a *map* where any chunk is related to any other chunk.

Chunks can be seen as information; data; or objects, such as people, equipment, or documentation. You can deal with a problem by recognizing and organizing its component chunks in ways that will help you make decisions and identify the important actions that will solve the problem. Viewing the problem or process as chunks will be useful when diagramming the current situation in Step 2 and when defining the problem statement in Step 1. You can solve problems by finding all the chunks, arranging them into meaningful patterns, and by focusing on the important parts.

Diagramming the Current Situation

With these diagramming principles, you should be ready to draw your first diagram or elaborate on the high-level flowchart created in Step 1. An iterative approach is recommended where the flowchart is drawn and redrawn until the cross-functional team reaches a consensus:

1. Begin by drawing a high-level process diagram or flowchart using ideas collected during brainstorming among the team members and from discussions outside the team environment with management, subject matter experts, and users.

2. Redraw the process diagram or flowchart as needed.

3. Take a vote and obtain consensus of the current situation diagram.

For example purposes, I have selected a flowchart from my current book *Achieving 100% Compliance of Policies and Procedures* (see Figure 3-2 below). This flowchart is based on a case study and task list; the case study is used as the primary example throughout the book.

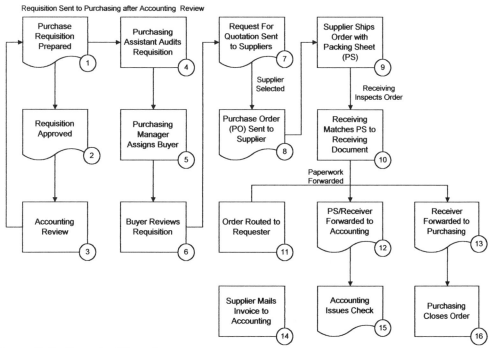

Figure 3-2: Sample Flowchart

Additional interviews and discussions with process owners could be needed to insure the process flow is adequately defined. After the flowchart has been completed, the cross-functional team should perform a walk-through to insure that the process in the flowchart and summary description match the real situation, as seen through the eyes of those doing the work. Missing information can be added to the flowchart, and gaps in the flow can be further researched through interviews with users and process owners.

A "task list" (refer to case study in *Achieving 100% Compliance of Policies and Procedures*) can be developed to document the details of the flowchart. Each block on the flowchart is numbered and corresponds to a task list that describes each block. The use of the task list makes the conversion process (from flowchart or data into a policy or procedure document) much easier than trying to interpret information from a flowchart as you write the policy or procedure document. As you will see, a task list can be used as an intermediary step between the flowchart and the policy or procedure document. In many cases, the task list can easily be converted into the "Procedures" section of the writing format. When research is completed and the team agrees that all refinements are completed, Step 5 ends and Step 6, "Document Solution," begins.

STEP 3: IDENTIFY & DIAGRAM ALTERNATIVE SOLUTIONS

The selection of alternative solutions is an important part of the team meeting experience. This is the fun part of the meetings. This is the bridge between perceiving, defining, and analyzing a problem, and evaluating and deciding on a final solution. Thinking up alternatives to the original problem statement can be a lot of fun, particularly in group situations. The team can use a variety of resources to gather, explore, and develop solutions. This effort could take weeks or months depending on the complexity of the problem statement. More than likely, you will have already identified a number of solutions during your initial team meetings and brainstorming sessions. Sources that could aid in the identification of alternative solutions include:

- Brainstorming sessions
- Subject matter experts
- Managers and users
- Vendors or suppliers
- Internal or external benchmarking
- Business process reengineering techniques
- Flowcharting and a gap analysis
- Existing documentation

- ◆ Books and journals
- ◆ Automation
- ◆ Internet research

Once you have defined the problem statement and created a diagram of the current situation, you are ready to generate alternative solutions. The same techniques you used for diagramming the initial problem (Steps 1 and 2) can be used for diagramming each alternative solution. A single solution is selected in Step 4, "Choose One Solution."

STEP 4: CHOOSE ONE SOLUTION

Selecting a single solution from among alternative solutions is an important decision for the cross-functional team. Teams often have trouble bringing closure and reaching a final decision. There are several decision-making tools for selecting a solution from a list of alternatives: voting, consensus, and matrix decision-making using a criteria-rating form. The first two tools produce a subjective result; the third produces an objective result based on a subjective ranking system. This last method is preferred, though you will still use either voting or consensus decision-making tools for deciding on which components to use on the criteria rating form. While there are other methods for making decisions (for example, paired choice or scenario thinking), you should limit your choices and not complicate the decision-making process.

VOTING

The quickest and easiest way to make a decision is to ask for a show of hands and settle on the solution that receives the most votes.

CONSENSUS

Consensus is the preferred *subjective* decision-making method because it requires that everyone agree to a selected alternative solution, to some extent. Everyone may not agree on every detail, but team members do believe that the selected solution is a sound decision, and they are willing to support it.

CRITERIA RATING FORM

A *criteria rating form* is an interpretation and ranking tool you can use to select ideas and solutions from among several alternatives. This decision-making tool is best used when you want to select among several alternatives, make a decision objectively, or agree on a decision. Richard Y. Chang, author of

Continuous Improvement Tools – Volume 1, introduced this form. Chang's *Volume 1* is an excellent book, and I also recommend you read his second volume. Refer to the "References" section at the end of this chapter for more information. There are six steps used to create a criteria-rating form:

1. *List Alternatives Available:* Gather the list of alternative solutions.

2. *Select Criteria*: Select decision criteria. Common criteria include:

    ♦ Compatibility with vision and strategic direction
    ♦ Ability to meet customer requirements
    ♦ Lowest cost and risk
    ♦ Flexibility, long-term workability, and ease of implementation
    ♦ Resource availability

3. *Select Weighting Factor*: Determine the relative importance of each criterion. To determine the weight of each criterion, ask, "How important is each of the criterion in relationship to the others?" The effectiveness of the criteria rating process is heavily dependent upon the weighting of the criteria. For this reason, the weighting decisions must be made by a team with input from all members. For unbiased input, ask each team member to weigh the criteria individually. Determine the final weight by averaging the individual weights assigned by each team member. The total of the assigned weights for all criteria must equal 100 percent.

4. *Rate Alternatives*: Establish a rating scale and rate the alternatives. Use a rating scale with 10 as the highest and 1 as the lowest. The team must use a consistent rating scale to compare various alternatives against each criterion. Any scale will work as long as you use the same scale for all alternatives and criteria. Each alternative solution should be rated against each criterion using the established rating scale.

5. *Calculate Final Score*: Calculate the final score by multiplying the weighting factor by the rating for each alternative (the rating scale).

CASE STUDY

I have selected an example of a criteria-rating form (Figure 3-3) based on the case study presented in my current book, *Achieving 100% Compliance of Policies and Procedures*. This case study started with a problem statement whereby employees were using a manual purchase requisition form to request the purchase of goods and services. Employees discovered that they could get their purchases faster by bypassing the purchasing department using a personal credit card or check, company check, or cash. The problem was to find a way to get the employees to want to use the tools provided by the purchasing system.

For the purposes of this example, four alternative solutions were selected: Purchase Card, Blanket Order, Web-based Ordering, and Electronic Data Interchange (EDI). Each of these alternatives is discussed in detail in the full case study in *Achieving 100% Compliance of Policies and Procedures*. The criteria rating form has been selected to help the procedures analyst determine which alternative is best. The numbers are fictitious and show one possible outcome when using the criteria rating form.

Criteria	Weighting Factor	Alternative Solutions			
		Purchase Card	Blanket Order	Web-based Ordering	EDI
Reduce paperwork	40%	9 x .4 (3.6)	2 x .4 (.8)	8 x .4 (3.2)	10 x .4 (4.0)
Increase productivity	10%	10 x .1 (1.0)	5 x .1 (.5)	10 x .1 (1.0)	8 x .1 (.8)
Tighten approvals	10%	9 x .1 (.9)	5 x .1 (.5)	9 x .1 (.9)	9 x .1 (.9)
Lower cost	25%	10 x .25 (2.5)	2 x .25 (.5)	7 x .25 (1.75)	2 x .25 (.5)
Lower risk	5%	8 x .05 (.40)	3 x .05 (.15)	7 x .05 (.35)	8 x .05 (.40)
Ease of implementation	10%	9 x .1 (.9)	8 x .1 (.8)	10 x .1 (1.0)	1 x .1 (.10)
Total	100%	9.3	3.25	8.2	6.7
RESULTS		1st Choice	4th Choice	2nd Choice	3rd Choice

Figure 3-3: Criteria Rating Form

Note: The calculation for each alternative solution uses the following formula (Rating Scale x Weighting Factor). For example, for "reduce paperwork," the calculation is Rating Factor (9) x Weighting Factor (.4) with a result of 3.6.

6. *Select Best Alternative*: In the case study, when the math is applied to each alternative solution, the best choice is the Purchase Card, with Web-based Ordering close behind. While the development of this form could have several iterations, I simplified the process and only displayed the final results. For more information, review Richard Chang's *Continuous Improvement Tools* books. Before making the final section, double-check your work and ask the question: "Do the results make intuitive sense based on the criteria and knowledge of each alternative solution?" If not, recheck the rankings, weights, and arithmetic.

Regardless of the decision-making tool (voting, consensus, criteria rating form) used by the cross-functional team, one alternative solution must be selected. The team should avoid the worse case scenario where it cannot reach a consensus, and, as a result, a manager or sponsor outside the team environment is asked to make a decision. The procedures analyst should insist that the team members reach a decision; if necessary, he should even make compromises to ensure that an alternative solution is selected before moving to Step 5, "Refine Solution."

STEP 5: REFINE SOLUTION

The purpose of this step is to put a little extra effort into the selected alternative solution to get it ready to be transformed into a policy or procedure document. Step 5 is a combination of Steps 1-4. In Step 1, the problem statement is identified and a high-level diagram is created. In Step 2, a detailed diagram is created for the current situation. In Step 3, alternative solutions are identified and diagrammed. In Step 4, one alternative solution is selected and becomes the input to Step 5.

This fifth step is used to refine the diagrams produced in Steps 1-3 and to begin the documentation process for the policy or procedure document. The procedures analyst should use any of the methods and tools introduced in Steps 1-3 to further refine the selected solution. This step is a good place to introduce the alternative brainstorming techniques mentioned earlier in the chapter. The goal of this step is to finalize any diagrams and content necessary to begin writing the policy or procedure document. Any changes or improvements should take place in this step. The procedures analyst can start the process of asking team members to make contributions to sections of the writing format. The procedures analyst should take the initiative and teach the team members how to use the writing format and give guidance as to what goes into each of the seven sections. The writing format is introduced in *Establishing a System of Policies and Procedures* and is carried through each of my books as the primary method for structuring and documenting printed and electronic (network and web) policies and procedures The writing format is the focus of Chapter 4, "Writing Policies and Procedures" and of my book, *7 Steps to Better Written Policies and Procedures*.

STEP 6: DOCUMENT SOLUTION

While this step is the subject of Chapter 4, I mention it because it is the last step of the problem-solving process introduced earlier in this chapter. The purpose of this step is to finish writing the policy or procedure document that was started in

Step 5 and publish the document. The team members have the following responsibilities in this step:

1. Finish writing the policy or procedure document that was started in Step 5.

2. Assist the procedures analyst with the coordination of the completed policy or procedure document with users and management for review purposes.

3. Assist the procedures analyst with the publication, communications, and training of the policy or procedure document.

4. Champion the new or revised policy or procedure document to employees that work in your department.

Refer to my book *Achieving 100% Compliance of Policies and Procedures* for details about effective communication, training, and mentoring plans. Separate chapters cover communications and training/mentoring plans.

DISBANDING
THE TEAM

Cross-functional teams are usually formed to handle one or two topics. When the topics are transformed into policies and procedures, published, and communicated, the team can be disbanded, or split apart. You might be asking: "Why do you disband the team?" "Why not keep the same team for the research and development of all policies and procedures for a specific company manual?" These are good questions. The answer is two-fold: First, the procedures analyst does not want to disband the team—he would like to keep the team members available for future work on policies and procedures for similar areas. However, retaining the employees may not be a choice for the procedures analyst. The team member's functional manager may have loaned his employees for a set purpose or period of time. Second, few policies and procedures cover the same functional areas. The procedures analyst will want to form new cross-functional teams to handle different functional areas. He has the goal of producing the best, most understandable, and most used policies and procedures. By using different people with different skill sets for each cross-functional team, the procedures analyst can achieve a wider span of customer buy-in and commitment. The procedures analyst might use some of the same people from team to team, but it makes more sense to choose new people as new topics are selected from the draft table of contents.

REVISIONS TO POLICIES
AND PROCEDURES

While this book focuses on writing new policies and procedures, the same problem-solving methods and tools can be applied to revising existing policies and procedures. My current book on policies and procedures, *Achieving 100% Compliance of Policies and Procedures*, shows the procedures analyst how to improve policies and procedures through communications, training, mentoring, review, compliance, auditing, and process improvement methods and tools. This book is a good teaching tool for members of a cross-functional team because it is based on a case study that demonstrates how to use quality tools to improve a procedure.

H. James Harrington, author of *Business Process Improvement*, suggests the use of 12 streamlining tools for the improvement of business processes, policies, and procedures. These tools could be used when diagramming alternatives to the current problem statement and when refining the selected solution in Step 4. Streamlining suggests the trimming of waste and excess and attention to every detail that might lead to improved performance and quality. A primary goal of revising policies or procedures is to make improvements to the business processes. These 12 streamlining tools follow:

- Bureaucracy elimination
- Duplication elimination
- Value-added assessment
- Simplification
- Process cycle-time reduction
- Error proofing
- Upgrading
- Simple language
- Standardization
- Supplier partnerships
- Big picture improvement
- Automation and/or mechanization

According to H. James Harrington, *"These tools are proven techniques. In fact, some have been so successful in business and industry the past three decades that they have evolved into entire disciplines."* He continues, *"When you use these methods consistently, your improvement potential and actual accomplishments are multiplied several times over."*

CHECKLIST FOR UNDERSTANDING

1. A plan of action is created to schedule work on a topic that has been selected by the procedures analyst from the prioritized table of contents pages prepared in Chapter 2, "Building Table of Contents Pages."

2. A cross-functional team is created and team members are selected to transform a selected topic from the initial problem statement to a published policy or procedure document.

3. The cross-functional team uses a six-step problem-solving process to define a problem, diagram the current situation, identify and diagram alternative solutions, choose a solution, refine the solution, and document the solution.

4. The cross-functional team begins to populate the writing format (policy or procedure document) during Step 5 "Refine Solution."

5. The team is disbanded when the cross-functional team accomplishes its goal of publishing and communicating a policy or procedure.

6. The techniques presented in this chapter can also be used when revising policies and procedures.

REFERENCES

Barner, Robert W., *Team Troubleshooting*, Davies-Black Publishing, Palo Alto, California. 2000.

Bass, Lawrence W., *Management by Task Forces*, Lomond Books, Mt. Airy, Maryland, 1975.

Blanchard, Kenneth, Ph.D; Carew, Donald, Ed.D, Pariss-Carew, Eunice, Ed.D, *The One Minute Manager Builds High Performing Teams*, William Morrow and Company, Inc., New York, New York, 1990.

Brilhart, John K. and Galanes, Gloria J., *Effective Group Discussion*, Wm. C. Brown Publishers, Dubuque, Iowa, 1989.

Carr, Clay, *Team Power*, Prentice-Hall, Englewood Cliffs, New Jersey, 1992.

Catapult Inc., *Step by Step Microsoft Project 98*, Microsoft Press, Redmond, Washington, 1996.

Chang, Richard Y, and Niedzwiecki, Matthew E., *Continuous Improvement Tools – Volumes 1 and 2*, Richard Chang Associates, Inc., Irvine, California, 1997.

Davenport, Thomas H., *Process Innovation*, Harvard Business School Press, Boston, Massachusetts, 1993.

Doyle, Michael and Straus, David, *How to Make Meetings Work*, Jove Books, New York, New York, 1976.

Fink, Arlene and Kosecoff, Jacqueline, *How to Conduct Surveys*, Sage Publications, Inc., Thousand Oaks, California, 1998.

Fisher, Kimball; Rayner, Steven; Belgard, William, *Tips for Teams*, McGraw-Hill, New York, New York, 1995.

Frank, Milo, *How to Run a Successful Meeting in Half the Time*, Simon and Schuster, New York, New York, 1989.

Harrington, H. James, *Business Process Improvement*, McGraw-Hill, Inc., New York, New York, 1991.

Harrington-Mackin, Deborah, *Keeping the Team Going*, AMACOM, New York, New York, 1996.

Heller, Robert and Hindle, Tim, *Essential Manager's Manual*, DK Publishing, Inc., New York, New York, 1998.

Hughes, Richard L, Ginnett, Robert C., Curphy, Gordon J., *Leadership*, Irwin/McGraw Hill, Boston, Massachusetts, 1996.

Jones, Morgan D., *The Thinker's Toolkit*, Three Rivers Press, New York, New York, 1995.

Kelsey, Dee and Plumb, Pam, *Great Meetings! How to Facilitate Like a Pro*, Hanson Park Press, Portland, Maine, 1999.

Krueger, Richard A. and Casey, Mary Ann, *Focus Groups*, Sage Publications, Inc., Thousand Oaks, California, 2000.

Lewis, James P., *How to Build and Manage a Winning Project Team*, American Management Association, New York, New York, 1993.

Lucas, Robert William, *The Big Book of Flip Charts*, McGraw-Hill, Inc., Boston, Massachusetts, 2000.

Page, Stephen B., *7 Steps to Better Written Policies and Procedures*, BookMasters, Inc., Mansfield, Ohio, 2001.

Page, Stephen B., *Achieving 100% Compliance of Policies and Procedures*, BookMasters, Inc., Mansfield, Ohio, 2000.

Page, Stephen B., *Establishing a System of Policies and Procedures*, BookMasters, Inc., Mansfield, Ohio, 1998.

Parker, Glenn M., *Cross-Functional Teams*, Jossey-Bass Publishers, San Francisco, California, 1994.

Payne, Vivette, *The Team-Building Workshop*, American Management Association, New York, New York, 2001.

Pell, Arthur, R., Ph.D, *The Complete Idiot's Guide to Team Building*, Alpha Books, Indianapolis, Indiana, 1999.

Peterson, Robert A., *Constructing Effective Questionnaires*, Sage Publications, Inc., Thousand Oaks, California, 2000.

Roth, William F., Jr., *Problem-Solving for Managers*, Praeger Special Studies, New York, New York 1985.

Straker, David, *Rapid Problem Solving with Post-It*® Fisher Books, Tucson, Arizona, 1997.

Willcocks, Graham, and Morris, Steve, *Successful Team Building*, Barron's, Hauppauge, New York, 1997.

Zey, Michael G., *The Mentor Connection*, Transaction Publishers, New Brunswick, New Jersey, 1991.

Chapter 4

Writing Policies and Procedures

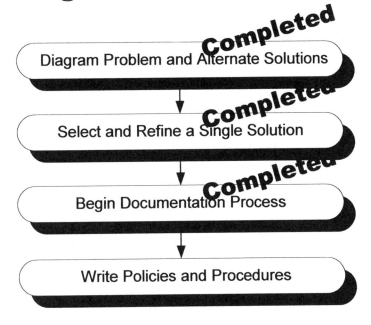

CHAPTER FOCUS

This chapter focuses on the transformation of ideas, text, and diagrams into a policy or procedure document using a structured writing format. A writing process is introduced that helps the procedures analyst coordinate the draft policy or procedure through the review and approval process. While developing the policies and procedures actually begins in Chapter 3, "Developing Policies and Procedures," the details for writing the policy or procedure document are included in this chapter. By this time, the table of contents has been drafted, the cross-functional team has been created, and the team has used a problem-solving process to define a problem, select a solution, and begin populating the sections of the writing format with relevant content. The writing format is introduced in my first book *Establishing a System of Policies and Procedures* and is an integral part of my current books on policies and procedures. As my other books contain extensive information on the writing format, the information in this chapter will be an overview of the principles and guidelines for using a structured writing format. My third book *7 Steps to Better Written Policies and Procedures* is a workbook devoted exclusively to the writing format; it provides step-by-step instructions for consistently filling the seven sections of the writing format with information gathered during the research and development phases of writing policies and procedures.

THE WRITING FORMAT

The Merriam-Webster's Collegiate Dictionary defines the term *format* as "a general plan of organization or arrangement." This term applies perfectly to writing policies and procedures because the structure, arrangement, and organization of process and procedural information are essential for understanding the content of policies and procedures.

> Think of a writing format as a way to present your policies and procedures in a consistent and structured format each and every time.

The task of standardizing the organization of policies and procedures is divided into two steps: (1) grouping similar subjects and (2) linking those groups logically. The arrangement of these two steps is determined by a third factor, a writing format. The phrase *writing format* can be defined as "an organized plan for writing structured policy and procedure documents."

OVERVIEW

The hallmark of a successful writing format is a standard structure, explicit section headings, and consistent and accurate content. The writing format is the heart of a system of policies and procedures because it provides a structure for information collected during the research and development phases of writing. A logical, structured writing format is a basic requirement for a policy or procedure. This method of writing helps to convert ideas and concepts into structured paragraphs, sentences, and words.

The significance of the writing format cannot be overemphasized. In absence of a writing format, the policies and procedures could not be formalized—the policies and procedures would remain unstructured thoughts in the heads of those making decisions. A system of policies and procedures is doomed to a slow death if procedure writers are permitted to publish policies and procedures in a different way each time, without structure. The main purpose of the writing format is to give you a means by which to express your ideas in a logical, structured, meaningful, and documented manner. All policies and procedures should use the same format or template to assure consistency of structure and organization. As a result, your policies and procedures should be comprehensive, easy-to-read, and easy-to-apply.

FLEXIBILITY OF THE WRITING FORMAT

The writing format is flexible and can be applied to any policy or procedure document. The only rigidity is in the number of sections. There are seven sections—no more, no less. Each section within the writing format is written as an outline, unless there is good reason to write it differently. Consistent section headings from document to document save time because readers can quickly find the information they need and focus on content rather than format. More importantly, consistency coupled with informative section headings encourages the reader to believe that the document he is holding (or viewing on a computer) is a quality document and deserves attention.

The writing format contains three types of information: (1) identification information such as title, identification number, effective date, revision date, page numbers, and approval signatures; (2) body, or content, of the policy or procedure; and (3) optional documentation (for example, form examples and instructions, diagrams, or tables) that could be included at the end of the policy or procedure document. While the body and optional documentation are viewed as the content of a policy or procedure document, the identification information can be viewed as the format, or framework, that houses the content.

The writing format is written in an outline style with seven standard section headings. The writing format has seven sections, no more, no less. The headings are self-explanatory and arranged in a logical sequence, beginning with a "Purpose" section and concluding with a "Procedures" section. These headings provide information and visual breaks to reveal the structure of your text, thus making it easy to locate information and follow the process flow. If these section headings were arranged differently from one time to the next, the reader would find it difficult to stay focused and understand the intent of the document. By using an unchanging sequence of section headings, the reader can stay focused as he reads through a policy or procedure.

The seven sections of the writing format are:

1. Purpose

2. Revision History

3. Persons Affected

4. Policy

5. Definitions

6. Responsibilities

7. Procedures

These headings will always appear in the sequence presented above for policies and procedures. The only difference in content between a policy and a procedure is that the policy usually does not contain content under the seventh heading, "Procedures."

USING THE WRITING FORMAT

The writing format is an excellent tool because you can collect information sequentially or randomly. In both cases, when you have completed the seven sections, you will have a logical and coherent document. There are two methods for populating the section headings of the writing format. First, you can add the information all at once. Somewhat like free writing, the principle is to capture as much information as possible and keep writing until you have completed filling in the seven section headings. Second, you can complete the section headings in any sequence. You can give specific sections to team members to complete. I often use the term *bucket* when referring to each section. The idea is to fill the buckets with information. This is an easy way for cross-functional team members to view the writing process. Each member can add to sections of the writing format. The procedures analyst can put the finishing touches on the draft and resubmit it to the cross-functional team for review. The procedures analyst has the important role of coordinating the draft policy or procedure with users and management, including publishing and training. This second approach is useful when the document is large and affects many functions or groups.

A well-written document makes its point quickly, and efficiency is achieved because a reader can understand the primary goals and objectives of a policy or procedure after reading just a few pages! Many readers are only interested in a summary view of the policy or procedure. Others want to know the details so that they can apply the principles and processes to their daily work life. You will appreciate the simplicity of the writing format when you become comfortable with its use and application. Transforming content into a structured writing format can become straightforward and easy.

#	Section Heading
1.0	Purpose: Objectives for writing a policy or procedure. Two or three sentences are adequate for this introductory paragraph.
2.0	Revision History: History of document changes, whether they are minor typographical errors, major improvements, or re-engineering efforts.
3.0	Persons Affected: List of persons or groups that might influence or support a specific policy or procedure.
4.0	Policy: General organizational attitude of an organization; a policy statement reflects the basic objectives, vision, strategic direction, core processes, attitudes, or culture.
5.0	Definitions: Provides explanations of abbreviations, acronyms, words frequently used, jargon, and technical terms. Optional documentation is also defined, for example, forms, standards, diagrams, models, or reports.
6.0	Responsibilities: Short summary of the roles and responsibilities of the individuals who perform the actions of a policy or procedure. This section should be written in the same sequence of events that occurs under the "Procedures" section in a procedure document.
7.0	Procedures: The process for accomplishing the purpose. The process is described from start to finish, including all inputs, outputs, and value-added activities. This section should follow the sequence of the flowchart and task list created during cross-functional team meetings.
	Optional Documentation: Forms, diagrams, models, flowcharts, and cumbersome text can be referenced either at the end of a policy or procedure or at an external location. A corresponding definition should be included in Section 5.0.

Table 4-1: Writing Format Layout

The writing format is to be used exactly as illustrated above. The numbering system and the use of underlined words are constant. Optional documentation is not a section heading; it refers to documentation that is attached to the policy or procedure or that exists in an outside location.

ALIGNING POLICIES AND PROCEDURES TO THE ALIGNMENT CONTINUUM

The alignment of the policies and procedures to any of the components of the alignment continuum (vision, strategic plan, core processes, or policies and procedures) can be a straightforward process. The alignment of policies and procedures is best accomplished in the "Purpose" and "Policy" sections, as these two sections should describe the purpose and rationale for a policy or procedure document. The "Procedures" section can also be used. Your references can take the form of "keywords" or "phrases" extracted from the vision, strategic plan, or core processes of an organization.

For purposes of an example, we will look at the DuPont vision statement published on the Internet (April, 2002). Their vision reads:

We, the people of DuPont, dedicate ourselves daily to the work of improving life on our plant.

We have the curiosity to go farther … the imagination to think bigger … the determination to try harder … and the conscience to care more.

Our solutions will be bold. We will answer the fundamental needs of the people we live with to ensure harmony, health and prosperity in the world.

Our methods will be our obsession. Our singular focus will be to serve humanity with the power of all the sciences available to us.

Our tools are our minds. We will encourage unconventional ideas, be daring in our thinking, and courageous in our actions. By sharing our knowledge and learning from one other and the markets we serve, we will solve problems in surprising and magnificent ways.

Our success will be ensured. We will be demanding of ourselves and work relentlessly to complete our tasks. Our achievement will create superior profits for our shareholders and ourselves.

Our principles are sacred. We will respect nature and living things, work safely, be gracious to one another and our partners, and each day we will leave for home with consciences clear and spirits soaring.

DuPont's Vision
(http://www.dupont.com/corp/overview/glance/vision/index.html)

There are several ways to use this vision. You can select a key phrase and paraphrase it, you can select a few key words, or you can simply reference the vision in your policy or procedure document. For example if you are writing a "Procurement Policy," you could write, "This procurement process will help us achieve superior profits for our employees and customers" and include the sentence in the "Policy" section. Note the phrase "superior profits" in the second to last paragraph in the vision. You can choose any word or phrase you deem appropriate. For example, the phrases, "improving life," "ensuring harmony," "sharing our knowledge," or "respecting others" could be used in most policies or procedures. The easiest alignment technique is to state the following: "This policy reflects our corporate vision." Or similarly, "This procedure reflects the goals of our corporate strategic plan." Both of these statements could be incorporated into the "Purpose" or "Policy" section of a policy or procedure document.

You might be wondering, now what? Once the procedures analyst is certain that the policies and procedures reflect the content of one or more of the alignment continuum components, he should advertise that the organization's system of policies and procedures supports the organization's purpose and direction. This kind of communication can only help the procedures analyst achieve management commitment and compliance of the policies and procedures.

THE WRITING PROCESS

The writing process is a system of five steps for coordinating the policy or procedure draft from idea initiation to publication. The process involves doing preparatory work; converting ideas into paragraphs, sentences, and words; editing the draft; coordinating reviews and approvals; and publishing the policy or procedure document. The writing process has five steps:

1. Prewriting

2. Preparing the First Draft

3. Editing Subsequent Drafts

4. Coordinating Reviews and Approvals

5. Publishing the Approved, Final Document

The task of writing policies and procedures uses a method of business writing that is a combination of formal and informal writing. Unlike formal business correspondence, grammar and punctuation do not always follow all the rules. Word processors have blurred the distinction between writing and editing. The once sharply defined steps of writing, analyzing, and revising can now be integrated into a more smoothly flowing whole: You can revise as you write, and write as you revise. Even though the first four steps of the writing process overlap, each step should be treated as a distinct process when writing and publishing policies and procedures. The fifth step is likely to stand on its own.

When the solution is selected (Chapter 3, "Developing Policies and Procedures"), the prewriting step can begin. The term *prewriting* refers to efforts to document and diagram a business process and to prepare to transform the information into a draft policy or procedure. Prewriting is about finding or creating the content for the topics selected for policy and procedure documents. The second and third steps, "preparing the first draft" and "editing subsequent drafts," begin when the solution has been diagrammed and a task list (detailed list of tasks extracted from a flowchart) has been created. The procedures analyst can introduce the writing format at this time. This process should be straightforward, especially if you use the "buckets" concept of filling in the information. The fourth and fifth steps, "coordinating reviews and approvals" and "publishing the approved, final document," begin with the draft of a policy or procedure document and conclude with a published policy or procedure. Refer to my current book *Establishing a System of Policies and Procedures* for details about coordinating the review process and obtaining approvals, and for publishing the completed and approved policy or procedure document. Once a policy or procedure is published, the writing process stops, and the compliance plan, improvement activities, and the revision process begin. Refer to my book *Achieving 100% Compliance of Policies and Procedures* for details about the compliance plan and improvement activities and to my book *7 Steps to Better Written Policies and Procedures* for details about the writing process and editing checklists.

CHECKLIST FOR UNDERSTANDING

1. The ultimate goal of the cross-functional team is to transform a defined and refined solution into a structured policy or procedure document using the writing format. The team will use problem-solving techniques for defining a problem, diagramming a current problem and alternate solutions, selecting and refining a single solution, and transforming the content into a policy or procedure document. The procedures analyst will use the writing process to coordinate the flow of documents from the idea phase to the publication of the policies and procedures.

2. A seven-section writing format is introduced for achieving efficient, consistent, and coherent policies and procedures. Methods for using the writing format are detailed. The exact layout of the writing format, including short descriptions, is illustrated.

3. A process for aligning policies and procedures to the alignment continuum components (vision, strategic plan, and core processes) is demonstrated with

the use of an example from the DuPont website whereby specific keywords and phrases of the vision are incorporated into the "Policy" section of a policy or procedure document.

4. The procedures analyst is responsible for coordinating the review of the policy or procedure document with team members, management, subject matter experts, sponsors, users, and others, as deemed needed by the cross-functional team.

5. Upon completion of the review process, the policy or procedure document can be approved, published, communicated, and trained.

REFERENCES

Bates, Jefferson, D., *Writing with Precision, Sixth Edition*, Acropolis Books LTD, Washington, D.C., 1993.

Cormier, Robin A., *Error-Free Writing*, Prentice-Hall, Englewood Cliffs, New Jersey, 1995.

Dobrian, Joseph, *Business Writing Skills*, AMACOM, New York, New York, 1998.

Page, Stephen B., *7 Steps to Better Written Policies and Procedures*, BookMasters, Inc., 2001.

Page, Stephen B., *Achieving 100% Compliance of Policies and Procedures*, BookMasters, Inc., 2000.

Page, Stephen B., *Establishing a System of Policies and Procedures*, BookMasters, Inc., 1998.

Sorenson, Sharon, *Webster's New World Student Writing Handbook*, Prentice Hall, New York, New York, 1992.

Chapter 5

Table of Contents Examples
And Policy/Procedure URLs

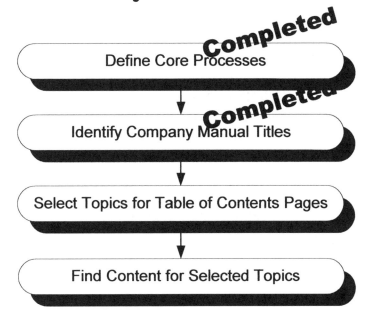

CHAPTER FOCUS

This chapter focuses on the process for finding content for tables of contents and policies and procedures. Figuring out where to start a company manual, what goes into a table of contents, what tools or resources to use for researching and developing policies and procedures, what processes are important to a specific policy or procedure, or where to find useful examples of policies and procedures are perplexing problems for anyone who has been assigned to write or revise policies and procedures.

> This chapter focuses on helping you find content for table of contents pages and for policy and procedure documents.

Short of providing thousands of policies and procedures that cover every possible process in every industry, this chapter has been designed to give you examples of tables of contents and policies and procedures from various organizational departments and industries. An extensive list of URLs are included that point to complete company manuals in many industries.

> The POWER of this book lies in the 50+ table of contents examples (15 complete tables of contents and over 40 table of contents URLs) and more than 150 policy/procedure URLs that point to thousands of real-life policies and procedures that are currently in use!

These examples and URLs will make your life easier because you no longer have to "re-invent the wheel" each time you want to start work on new or revised policies or procedures. You are shown easy ways to search the Internet to find content for the draft table of contents and to find content to fill the seven sections of the writing format for a policy or procedure document.

USING THE INTERNET TO FIND CONTENT

If you are seeking information about any process, policy, procedure, or information within those documents, the Internet is one of your best sources. Due to the success of the Internet as a source of information that anyone can access from almost anywhere, many entities (such as U.S. federal and state government agencies, universities, organizations, and some specialty websites) have selected the Internet as a place to store processes, policies, procedures, and other types of reference materials. Fortunately for us, these entities have placed tables of contents with URLs on the Internet that point to actual policies and procedures. You may be thinking: "Why would I be interested in tables of contents or policies and procedures published by organizations within different industries?" The answer is three-fold:

1. Policies and procedures are similar in nature across many industries and within many functional areas, or departments, and therefore can offer clues into the types of processes, policies, procedures, or documentation that may be needed for a system of policies and procedures. For example, purchasing and personnel departments are common functions in many industries and they adhere to similar rules and regulations regardless of the industry! Also, the way you do accounting or finance activities is similar from industry to industry due to industry-recognized accounting standards. By looking at how different organizations do similar functions, the procedures analyst can

often get a new perspective on the topics he is investigating. He can use this new information to enhance or support his current findings.

2. Table of contents and policy and procedure examples can offer insight into the kinds of questions that could be posed during the interviewing process when researching and developing policies and procedures. The examples can suggest the types of subjects covered by policies and procedures; these subjects can be used as a source of questions.

3. Potential external benchmarking partners may be discovered during your Internet searches.

I used to believe that policy and procedure examples would not be helpful because policies and procedures should be based on the culture, management direction, existing documentation or industry-specific standards and guidelines. I changed my views after discovering hundreds of examples of tables of contents and policies and procedures that could be used for reference purposes. I found that many of the processes and forms used in common functional areas (for example, accounting, finance, personnel, or purchasing) across industries are similar in content and format. I was surprised and pleased at the similarity of content. I strongly believe in networking and the sharing of ideas with my peers. This book was written so I could share my ideas, examples, and URLs with you. I hope that those who read this book will also feel compelled to share information with their peers.

USING TABLE OF CONTENTS EXAMPLES AND POLICY/PROCEDURE URLS

This chapter has been designed to help guide you in selecting and defining topics for table of contents pages and for defining the content for policies and procedures. I have included more than 150 URLs that point to thousands of real-life policies and procedures as well as to resources that will be helpful when you are researching and developing the topics selected from the draft table of contents.

Whether your organization is large or small, or if the individuals doing policies and procedures are novice writers or experienced professionals, these tables of contents and policies and procedures examples should prove useful and help reduce up front preparation and research time. These examples will provide insight into the different ways organizations write processes, policies, or procedures. Also, as some of these tables of contents are complete examples of common functional areas, the procedures analyst should feel quite comfortable using these extensive resources as background material when conducting interviews or brainstorming sessions.

SEARCHING THE INTERNET
FOR CONTENT

The Internet contains billions of websites and you can find almost anything you want if you have the patience. With the Internet, you can:

- ◆ Visit and print the information from websites for the table of contents and policy and procedure examples mentioned in this book. Follow the links and resources found at many of these websites.

- ◆ Search out additional table of contents pages, processes, policies, procedures, standards, or guidelines using keywords such as "table of contents," "policies and procedures," or "company manuals." For specific topics, use variations of keywords. For example, if you were seeking out policies and procedures on information technology, you might try keywords such as "information technology," "office of information technology," "information systems," "EDP," "data processing," or "management information systems."

- ◆ Search the URLs referenced in "Websites with Tons of Information," as these websites provide a wealth of information. As an added bonus, you will find that a few of the website owners are willing to communicate and share ideas with you. Look for those sites that offer "free information" or email addresses and start networking!

Do not overlook the Internet as a source of information. Even if you think you have the right information or enough information, I still recommend that you do searches on the Internet just to be sure that you are on the right track and/or to fill in possible gaps in your information.

For your convenience, I have gathered 15 complete table of contents examples, over 40 table of contents URLs, and more than 150 URLs that point to real-life policies and procedures and to useful resources that you can use in your research and development efforts. As I could not anticipate the needs of every procedures analyst, I have provided a sampling of some websites I have found on the Internet. I made it a point to areas common in multiple industries such as personnel, purchasing, accounting, or financial services. I also provided industry-specific table of contents examples such as childcare or hotel management to show you the diversity of content you can find on the Internet.

The table of contents examples and URLs have been developed from a number of sources, including actual company manuals, best practice resources, well-known authors and practioners, subject matter experts, Internet searches, benchmarking efforts, information technology consultants, and personal experience. To some, these lists will seem complete; to others, they will seem incomplete. In either case, I do recommend that you review the examples and URLs and make your own judgment as to their practicality.

LAYOUT OF EXAMPLES

The remainder of this chapter contains six sections. The first five sections contain references to URLs only. The sixth section contains fifteen examples of tables of contents, each with a URL reference to a corresponding company manual. These URLs are included on my website, which is located at *http://www.companymanuals.com/bestpractices/links.htm*. This web page contains all of the URLs mentioned in this book and some bonus references.

1. Functional Areas or Specialty Manuals (URLs)

2. Websites in this Book (URLs)

3. Websites with Tons of Information (URLs)

4. Standards Associations (URLs)

5. Table of Contents Examples (URLs)

6. Examples of Fifteen Tables of Contents

There are two ways to view these URLs: First, enter your browser and type the URL exactly as written in this chapter. This method is prone to typing errors. Second, visit *http://www.companymanuals.com/bestpractices/links.htm* and click on the hyperlink or "copy and paste" the URL into your browser. Clicking directly from the website is the preferred method. If you should decide to copy and paste the URL in your browser, be careful that you select only the URL, without any spaces on either side. If you notice any errors in the website, or wish to add URLs, please send me an email at *spage@columbus.rr.com*.

Using the URLs: Key in the exact URL as shown in the following pages or access my website that contains a "links" page at *http://www.companymanuals.com/bestpractices/links.htm.*

If the URL does not come up, then try one of the following options:

- Click your Refresh button
- Close your browser, reopen, and try entering the URL again
- Wait a few minutes and try entering the URL again
- Use the above LINKS URL
- Email me with the problem and I will assist you

Webmasters are continually changing and updating their websites. If you find any websites that have changed or reference a domain name that is no longer available, please email me and I will make a note of it for the next book reprint. I will also change it on the *links* website.

FUNCTIONAL AREAS or
SPECIALTY MANUALS (URLs)

Description: This table includes 15 common functional areas and specialty manuals and one or more URLs (40+ URLs). The entry in the first column corresponds to the first URL in the second column. The additional URLs in the second column are extra sources for the respective functional areas.

FUNCTIONAL AREAS / SPECIALTY MANUALS	URL http://
Accounting	*www.ucop.edu/ucophome/policies/acctman/* *www.pwcglobal.com/images/pwcerc/pdfs/acct-pol.pdf* *www.state.ak.us/local/akpages/ADMIN/dof/asksas/ aksas.htm*
Auditing	*www.unc.edu/depts/intaudit/CONTENTS.HTM*
Computer and Network Usage	*www.security.gatech.edu/*
Financial Services	*www.fin.uoguelph.ca/Manuals/Man-TOC.htm* *www.virginia.edu/~polproc/proc/Proc_toc.html*
Hotel Management	*www.marinmgmt.com/hotelmanuals.html*
Information Technology	*www.doit.ca.gov/simm/default.asp* *www.state.mi.us/cio/oits/* *www.state.ma.us/itd/spg/publications/standards/index.htm* *www.state.me.us/policybd/STANDARD/standard.htm* *www.state.me.us/policybd/POLICY/policy.htm* *http://olepe.icsd.hawaii.gov/dags/icsd/ppmo/ Stds_Web_Pages/MastTOC.htm* *http://cio.state.nm.us/itpolicies.htm* *http://psp.state.nv.us/psp.htm* *www.oit.state.ar.us/AgPlan/ITPlan_Home.asp* *www.state.sd.us/standards/index.htm* *www.state.tn.us/finance/oir/pol1.html* *www.mde.net/*
Library Services	*www.sirin.lib.il.us/docs/cen/docs/lib/tablecont.htm* *www.library.unt.edu/about/policies/toc.htm*
Medicare & Medicaid Programs (HCFA)	*www.hcfa.gov/pubforms/htmltoc.htm*
Nursing Manual	*www.health.state.mo.us/Publications/TBLEOFC.html* *www.uams.edu/nursingmanual/Policy/default.htm*

Patient Handbook	*www.stpetes.org/healserv/handbook.htm*
Personnel	*www.howardcc.edu/hr/policies/table_of_contents.htm*
	http://web.mit.edu/personnel/www/policy/
	www.state.ma.us/courts/admin/hr/tableofcontents.html
	www.sde.state.id.us/osbe/policy/SectionII.pdf
	www.state.co.us/hrs/
Project Management	*www.doit.ca.gov/simm/ProjectManagement/*
	ProjManagement.asp
	www.state.mi.us/cio/opm/
	www.unisys.com/marketplace/bookbeat/cmm/chart.html
Purchasing	*www.asu.edu/aad/manuals/pur/*
	www.uakron.edu/purchasing/manual/tableof.html
	www.uiowa.edu/~purchase/procurement/
	(Click on *Policy*)
Records Management	*http://osu.orst.edu/dept/archives/handbook/*
	www.dphhs.state.mt.us/policy/records_management.htm
	www2.state.id.us/adm/purchasing/recguide.PDF
Web Accessibility	*www200.state.il.us/tech/technology/accessibility/iwas1_2.htm*

WEBSITES IN THIS BOOK (URLs)

Description: This table outlines the websites included in this book. The information has been sorted by chapter.

CH.	SUBJECT AREAS	URL http://
Intro	Updated URLs	*www.companymanuals.com/bestpractices/links.htm*
Intro	Websites for Books by Stephen B. Page	*www.companymanuals.com/index.htm* *www.companymanuals.com/compliance/index.htm* *www.companymanuals.com/writingformat/index.htm* *www.companymanuals.com/bestpractices/index.htm*
1	Strategic Plans	*www.planware.org/strategy.htm*
2	ISO 9000 Series	*www.iso.ch/*
2	IEEE Practices	*www.ieee.org/*
2	Project Management Practices	*www.pmi.org/*
2	Capability Maturity Model	*www.sei.cmu.edu/sei-home.html*
2	State Website Format	*www.state.xx.us/* (where *xx* is a two-letter U.S. state code; for example, Ohio is OH or California is CA.)
2	Search Engines	*www.google.com* *www.yahoo.com* *www.looksmart.com* *www.hotbot.com* *www.askjeeves.com*
2	Benchmarking Sites	*www.benchmarking.org/* *www.benchmarkingreports.com/*
2	Association of Records Managers	*www.arma.org/*
2	Business Management Forms Association	*www.bfma.org/*
2	Associations Listing	*www.ipl.org/ref/AON/* (Scroll down to alphabetical listings for best results)
2	Electronic Books in Print	*www.bowkerlink.com/*
4	DuPont Vision	*www.dupont.com/corp/overview/glance/vision/* *index.html* *(Click on GLANCE and then on Vision Statement)*

WEBSITES WITH TONS OF INFORMATION (URLs)

Description: This table contains 25 websites of information that should prove useful for the research and development phase of writing policies and procedures. For example, if you are interested in technical or business resources, start with *http://www.tarrani.net*. If you are interested in software engineering subjects, start with *http://www.processimpact.com*.

TOPICS	URL http://
Amazon Bookstore	*www.amazon.com*
American Society of Quality	*www.asq.org/*
AuditNet	*www.auditnet.org/*
Audit Association	*www.isaca.org*
Benchmarking	*www.benchmarking.org/*
Best Practices Database	*www.bestpracticedatabase.com/*
Best Practices White Papers	*www.cisco.com/warp/public/126/*
Business Process Improvement	*www.c3i.osd.mil/org/bpr.html*
Capability Maturity Model (CMM)	*www.sei.cmu.edu/sei-home.html* *http://home.okstate.edu/homepages.nsf/toc/ level2.index.html* *www.davidfrico.com* *http://davidfrico.com/seiprocspdf.htm* *http://davidfrico.com/sei-lev-2-pols-procspdf.htm*
IEEE Bookstore	*http://shop.ieee.org/store/*
Informational Hot Link	*www.tantara.ab.ca/info.htm*
Quality Assurance Guidelines	*www.dir.state.tx.us/eod/qa/evaluate/*
Metrics	*www.industrymetrics.com*
Online IT Community	*www.gantthead.com* *www.techrepublic.com*
Personal Software Process	*http://davidfrico.com/psp-process-f.htm*
Process Definition Guidebook	*http://Source.asset.com/stars/loral/process/guide/ notation.htm*
Process Impact	*www.processimpact.com*
Project Management Bookstore	*www.pmibookstore.org/*
Quality Digest	*www.qualitydigest.com*

Six Sigma	*www.smartersolutions.com/html/articles.htm*
Software Engineering Resources	*www.rspa.com/spi/index.html*
Software Process Improvement	*www.davidfrico.com*
Software Quality Assurance Links	*www.ssq.org/* (Click on *Links* on the menu)
Software Testing	*www.testingstuff.com/testing2.html*
Technical and Business Resources	*www.tarrani.net/* *www.tarrani.net/linda/* *http://ZarateTarrani.blogspot.com/* *http://postcrds.blodspot.com/* *www.geocities.com/mtarrani/*

STANDARDS ASSOCIATIONS (URLs)

Description: This table contains 10 Standards Associations and corresponding URLs.

STANDARDS ASSOCIATIONS	URL http://
American Institute of Aeronautics and Astronautics (AIAA)	*www.aiaa.org/*
American National Standards Institute (ANSI)	*www.ansi.org/*
Canadian Standards Association (CSA)	*www.csa.ca/*
International Electrotechnical Commission (IEC)	*www.iec.ch/*
Electronic Industrial Association (EIA)	*www.eia.org/*
Institute of Electrical and Electronics Engineers, Inc. (IEEE)	*www.ieee.org/*
International Organization for Standardization (ISO)	*www.iso.ch/*
Joint Commission on Accreditation of Healthcare Organizations (JCAHO)	*www.jcaho.org/*
Project Management Institute (PMI)	*www.pmi.org/*
Software Engineering Institute (SEI)	*www.sei.cmu.edu/sei-home.html*

Moore, James W., Software Engineering Standards, *IEEE Computer Society,* Los Alamitos, California, 1998.

TABLE OF CONTENTS EXAMPLES (URLs)

Description: This table includes tables of contents for more than 40 examples of policy and procedure company manuals. I also have included some hard-to-find topics. The information in this table gives you an idea of what is available on the Internet when you take the time to look.

COMPANY MANUALS / POLICIES & PROCEDURES	URL http://
Administrative Policies and Procedures	www.mcg.edu/policies/
Airport Policies and Procedures	www.orlandoairports.net/goaa/content.htm
Banking	www.state.ct.us/dob/pages/dobtoc.htm
Child Care Manual	www.wvdhhr.org/oss/childcare/ (Click on *Child Care Policies* on the menu)
Church Policies and Procedures	www.adventist.org/churchmanual/ www.episcopalchurch.org/contents.html
Comptroller's Office	www.asu.edu/aad/manuals/com/index.html
Computer Security Administration	www.utoronto.ca/security/policies.html www.state.la.us./oit/security.htm www.security.state.az.us/policies.htm
Continuity Planning	www.security.state.az.us/continuity-planning.htm
Cost Accounting	www.rgs.uky.edu/ospa/costacc/casfac/
Credit Union Policies and Procedures	www.sheshunoff.com/products/creditunion/ creditunion.html
Criminal Justice	www.ncrle.net/jailtoc.htm *(Table of Contents Only, No URLs)*
Department of Public Safety	www.asu.edu/aad/manuals/dps/index.html
Desktop Standards	www.state.la.us/oit/desktop.htm
E-Services	www.state.la.us/oit/e_services.htm
Elections Policies and Procedures	www.co.whatcom.wa.us/auditor/Elections/ candidat/info/ElectionsPP/Policies/ Elections_p_p.htm
Email Policy	www.state.me.us/policybd/POLICY/interpol.htm
Emergency Medical Services	www.co.sacramento.ca.us/ems/toc.html
Facilities Management	www.east.asu.edu/admin/facilities.htm (If problems, type in the root http://www.asu.edu/aad/manuals/index.html and seek out the search feature)
Financial Administration	http://vpf-web.harvard.edu/documents/
Fiscal Management	www.cusys.edu/~policies/Fiscal/

Grant Accounting	*www.temple.edu/controller/*
Grant Administration	*www.odh.state.oh.us/About/Grants/ GAPManual/gapmanual.htm*
Infrastructure	*www.state.la.us/oit/infrastructure.htm*
Insurance Best Practices	*http://vpf-web.harvard.edu/rmas/4_insurance/ policies3.html*
Intercollegiate Athletes	*www.richmond.edu/athletics/manual/manlpre.htm*
Internet Use Policy	*www.state.me.us/policybd/POLICY/interpol.htm*
PC Standards	*www.state.sd.us/boa/computers/standards/ confgstd.htm*
Payroll Handbook	*http://osu.orst.edu/dept/budgets/payroll/paytoc.htm* *www.state.ak.us/local/akpages/ADMIN/dof/ aam/tocpay1.htm*
Power Plant Billing Procedures	*www.bpa.gov/Power/PSR/Billing_Procedures/ billing_procedures.htm*
Property Control Policies and Procedures	*www.Udri.udayton.edu/PropertyRecords/ contents.htm* *www.asu.edu/aad/manuals/pcs*
Proposal, Request For	*www.state.mt.us/doa/ppd/manualrfp.pdf*
Purchasing Card User Manual	*www.state.ak.us/local/akpages/ADMIN/dof/ pcard/manual.htm*
Risk Management	*www.asu.edu/aad/manuals/rsk/index.html*
Social Services	*www.dss.state.va.us/benefit/fs_manual.html*
Software Engineering Process Handbook	*http://Sw-eng.larc.nasa.gov/Guidebook/index.htm*
Telecommunications	*www.state.ak.us/local/akpages/ADMIN/info/ Guide/1_4ts.htm*
Training Manual	*http://crs.uvm.edu/nnco/cd/train2.htm*
Travel & Business Guidelines	*www.columbia.edu/cu/controller/* (Click Policies and Procedures on side bar)
University Governance	*http://Muweb.millersv.edu/~govern/*
University Policies and Procedures	*www.jmu.edu/jmupolicy/*
Various Manuals	*www.asu.edu/aad/manuals/index.html*

EXAMPLES OF FIFTEEN
TABLES OF CONTENTS

Description: The following pages contain 15 examples of table of contents pages (with policy or procedure titles) for the referenced topic. As I could not give "live" hyperlinks, the referring URL has been included for quick reference. Each item in the "Subject Area Category" and the "Detailed Subject Areas" columns should be hyperlinked text when you open the URL in your browser.

Each table starts on a new (odd-numbered) page and contains a single topic or company manual title, a functional area or industry that represents the topic, a "referring" URL, a subject area category (high-level topics); and detailed subject areas within the high-level topic.

TOPIC:	**Accounting Manual**
Functional Area:	**Any Industry**
http://www.ucop.edu/ucophome/policies/acctman/	
Subject Area Category	**Detailed Subject Areas**
Introduction	Copy Number Assignment
	List of Current Pages
	Table of Contents
	Index
	Foreword
	University Accounting Program
	Accounting Officers' Conferences
General	
A. Accounting Structure	Account Classification
	Accounting Codes: General Ledger
	Accounting Codes
	Uniform Accounting Structure
B. Accounting Records and Reports	Accounting Forms
	Accounting Records: Automatic Data Processing Entries
	Annual Reporting of Separate Entities
	Financial Control Accounts
	Financial Journals
	Official Documentation Required in

	Support of University Financial Transactions
	Reports
C. Other	Agency Accounts
	Delegation of Authority – Signature Authorization
	Insurance: Professional Medical and Hospital Liability Program
	Internal Control Standards
	Inventories
	Short-Term Investment Pool – Distribution of Income
	Use of State of California Pool Cars and Garage Facilities
Cost Accounting	Academic Support Unit Costing and Billing Guidelines
	University Direct Costing Procedures
Cash and Banking Transactions	Cash: Cash Controls
	Cash: Balances of Individual Funds
	Cash: Campus Cash Collection Deposits
	Cash: Check Controls
	Cash: Controlled Disbursements Processing
	Cash: Deposits and Other Credits
	Cash: Letters of Credit
	Cash: Petty Cash Disbursements
	Cash: Unclaimed and Uncashed Checks
	Cash: Credit and Debit Card Program
	Cashiering Responsibilities and Guidelines
	Procedures for Investigating Misuse of University Resources
	Internal Control Standards: Issuance and Control of Operating Cash Funds

Accounts Receivable Operations	Bankruptcy Claims
	Receivables Management
Accounts Payable Operations	
A. Disbursements	Disbursements: Advance Payments
	Disbursements: Approvals Required
	Disbursements: Cancellation and Redrawing of Vendor Checks
	Disbursements: Discount Terminology
	Disbursements: Encumbrance Accounting
	Disbursements: Freight
	Disbursements: Honorarium Payments
	Disbursements: Invoice Processing in Response to Purchase Authorizations
	Disbursements: Payments for Deceased Payees Made Through the Vendor System
	Disbursements: Use of Procurement Cards for Low-Value Purchases
B. Taxes	Disbursements: Accounting for and Tax Reporting of Payments Made Through the Vendor System
	Disbursements: State Tax Withholding from Non-Wage Payments to Non-Residents of California
	Tax Exemption and Refund Claims Filing for Property Leased by the University
	Taxes: Federal Excise Taxes
	Taxes: Federal Taxation of Aliens
	Taxes: Income Tax Information in the Accounting Manual
	Taxes: Sales and Use Tax
	Taxes: Taxpayer Identification Numbers
	Taxes: Transient Identification Numbers
	Taxes: State Fuel Taxes
	Taxes: Taxation of Scholarship and

	Fellowship Grants and Educational Assistance
	Taxes: Tax Withholding for States Outside of California
C. Other	Accounting and Reporting for Leases and Installment Purchase Contracts
	Administrative Fund Payments
	Assignments by Vendors and Construction Contractors
	Employee Non-Cash Awards
	Entertainment
	Senior Management Automobile Policy and Procedures
	Moving: Policy and Regulations Governing Moving and Relocation
	Reimbursement for Overtime Meals
	Travel: Policy and Regulations Governing Travel
Payroll Operations	
A. Gross Pay	Payroll: Attendance, Time Reporting, and Leave Accrual Records
	Payroll: Official Pay Dates
	Payroll: Damage Payments for Services Performed Before Loyalty Oath is Signed
	Payroll: Range Adjustments
B. Taxes	Payroll: Accounting for and Tax Reporting of Mandatory Deductions and Insurance Benefit Contributions
	Payroll: Federal Taxation of Citizens
	Payroll: Settlement Payments
	Payroll: State Tax Withholding from Employees
	Payroll: Federal Taxation of Aliens
	Payroll: Income Tax Information in the Accounting Manual

114

C. Retirements	Payroll: OASDI and Medicare Contributions
	Payroll: UCRS Accounting Procedures
D. Other Deductions and Benefits	Payroll: Contribution Deductions for Fund-Raising Organizations
	Payroll: Deduction-Cost Reimbursement
	Payroll: Group Automobile Insurance
	Payroll: Miscellaneous Payroll Deductions for Employee Organizations, Faculty Clubs, and Credit Unions
	Payroll: Unemployment Insurance
	Payroll: U.S. Savings Bonds
	Payroll: Workers' Compensation Insurance
E. Other	Internal Control Standards: Departmental Payrolls
	Payroll: Employee Death Payments
	Payroll: Intercampus Transfers and Appointments
	Payroll: Salary Attachments and Assignments
Student Financial Aid Operations	Accounting Procedures for Recording Federal Financial Aid Administrative Allowance
	Student Aid
	Student Aid: Economic Opportunity – Work Study Program
Current Funds Accounts	
A. General Funds	State Claims
B. Tuition Fees	Education Abroad Program: Intercampus Transactions
	Student Fees: Educational Fee
	Student Fees: Exemptions, Waivers, and Special Provisions

	University Extension Concurrent Courses
	University Extension: Summer Term Deferrals
C. Federal Government	Contracts and Grants: Cash Advance Programs
	Contracts and Grants: Federal Contract and Grant Administration Funds—Allocations for Administrative and Disallowed Costs
D. Special State Appropriations and Contracts	Contracts and Grants: Indirect Costs Recovered from State Agencies
E. Sales and Services of Educational Activities	Sales and Services of Educational Activities
F. Sales and Services of Auxiliary Enterprises	Accounting Procedures for Acquisition and Sale of Service Enterprise Assets
	Accounting Procedures for Funding Current Working Capital Requirements of Service Enterprises
	Auxiliary Enterprises
	Costing and Working Capital for Auxiliary and Service Enterprises
	Housing and Food Service Operations Uniform Cost Accounting System
G. Sales and Services of Teaching Hospitals	Health Care Services: Professional Fees
	Health Sciences Compensation Plans
	Hospitals: California Hospital Commission Accounting Manual
	Hospitals: Acquisition of Medical Groups
	Hospitals: Cost Reimbursement by Third Party Sponsors
	Hospitals: Financial Evaluation Standards
	Hospitals: Patient Activity and

	Financial Projections
	Hospitals: Plant Asset Accounting
	Hospitals: Reporting Requirements
	Hospitals: Clinical Teaching Support
	Hospitals: Working Capital
	Medical Centers
	Medical Centers: Medi-Cal Supplemental Payments
	Medical Centers: Patient Accounts Receivable
H. Other Sources	Campus Computer Center Fiscal Operations
	Computing Activities: Accounting Procedures for Campus Computer Centers
	Operating Guidelines for University Supply Inventories
Loan Fund Accounting	Employee Emergency Loan Fund
	Faculty Residential Mortgage Revenue Bond Programs
	Supplemental Home Loan Program
	Student Aid: Loan Fund Accounting
	Student Aid: William D. Ford Federal Direct Loan Program
Endowment and Similar Funds	Endowment and Similar Funds
	Investments and Investment Income
Plant Funds Accounting	
A. Unexpended Plant Funds	Plant Accounting: Borrowed Funds
	Plant Accounting: Housing Project Units for Sale to Faculty
	Plant Accounting: Fabricated Property
	Plant Accounting: Stop Notices, Assignments, and Tax Liens
	Plant Accounting: Unexpended Plant Funds

B. Retirement of Indebtedness Funds	Plant Accounting: Bond Financing
	Plant Accounting: Retirement of Indebtedness
C. Renewals and Replacements Funds	Plant Accounting: Renewals and Replacements
D. Investment in Plant Funds	Application of Proceeds from the Sale, Trade-in or Transfer of University Property
	Libraries and Collections: Capitalization
	Accounting and Reporting for Leases and Installment Purchase Contracts
	Plant Accounting: Capitalization of Expenditures Made from Current Funds
	Plant Accounting: Certifications of Participation
	Plant Accounting: Commercial Paper
	Plant Accounting: General Improvement Write-offs
	Plant Accounting: Investment In Plant
	Plant Accounting: State Capital Projects
	Recording Proceeds from the Sale, Trade-in or Transfer of University Property

TOPIC:	**Auditing**
Functional Area:	**University**
http://www.unc.edu/depts/intaudit/CONTENTS.HTM	

Subject Area Category	Detailed Subject Areas
Internal Audit Chapter	
Mission Statement	
Office Policies and Procedures	
On-Campus Parking	
Computer Policies	
Professional Standards	
Professional Proficiency	
Risk Assessment and Long Range Audit Plans	
Coordinating Work with External Auditors	
Scheduled Audits	
EDP Audits	
Special Projects, Management Requests	
Misuse Investigations	
Audit Follow-up Process	
Working Paper Documentation	
Communicating Results	
Confidentiality of Information	

TOPIC:	**Computer and Network Usage Policy**
Functional Area:	**Information Technology (IT)**
http://www.security.gatech.edu/	

Subject Area Category	Detailed Subject Areas
Preface	
Background and Purpose	
Definitions	Authorized Use
	Authorized Users
Individual Privileges	Privacy
	Ownership of Intellectual Works
	Freedom from Harassment and Undesired Information
Individual Responsibilities	Common Courtesy and Respect for Rights of Others
	Responsible Use of Resources
	Information Integrity
	Use of Personally Managed Systems
	Access to Facilities and Information
	Attempts to Circumvent Security
	Academic Honesty
	Use of Copyrighted Information and Materials
	Use of Licensed Software
	Political Campaigning; Commercial Advertising
	Personal Business
Tech Privileges	Allocation of Resources
	Control of Access to Information
	Imposition of Sanctions
	System Administration Access
	Monitoring of Usage; Inspection of Files
	Suspension of Individual Privileges

Technical Responsibilities	Risk Management
	Security Procedures
	Anti-Harassment Procedures
	Upholding of Copyrights and License Provisions
	Individual Unit Responsibilities
	Public Information Services
Procedures and Sanctions	Investigative Contact
	Responding to Security and Abuse Incidents
	First and Minor Incidents
	Subsequent and/or Major Violations
	Range of Disciplinary Sanctions
	Appeals
	Links to Applicable Policies and Procedures
Computer and Network Usage Policy	Microsoft Word Version
	Plain-Text Version

TOPIC:	**Financial Services**
Functional Area:	**Any Industry**
	*http://www.fin.uoguelph.ca/Manuals/Man-TOC.htm*

Subject Area Category	Detailed Subject Areas
Organization and Delegation	Introduction and Definition
	Financial Services Organization
Operating Fund	Travel Authority and Personal Claim Procedure
	Reimbursement of Hospitality Expense to University Members
	Allowances for University Employees Requested to Work at Locations Other than their Normal Place of Work
	Anti-Rabies Immunization
	University Payment of Faculty Club Invoices
	Requisition, Receiving, and Paying for Goods and Services
	Low Value Purchase Order System
	Forms Review/Printing and Register Control Systems
	Systems Contract Purchasing
	Coding Slips
	Cheque Requisition
	Payment of Honoraria and Travel Costs for Short-Term Visiting Professor Program
	Paperless Order Contract
	Purchasing, Receiving, Storing, and Disposal of Drugs Described in Food and Drugs Action and Regulations
	Internal Transfer Invoice for Intra-University Cost Transfers
	Telecommunication Charges
	Cost Recovery Policy and Procedure for Obtaining Instructional Support Services
	Declaration and Disposal of Surplus or Obsolete Furniture and Equipment

	Invoicing of Charges and Receipt of Cash by the Veterinary Teaching Hospital
Ancillary Enterprises	Collection of Student Telephone Tolls
	Collection and Control of Revenue Family Housing
Specific Purpose Funds	Research Grant in Lieu of Salary
	Cost Estimating and Other Procedures for University Contracts and Proposals
	Handling Animal Purchases from Research Grants
Cash and Investments	Control of Revenue by University Departments
	Control of Applications for Admission Pre-Veterinary Year
	Central Box Office Operations Control
	University Building Key System
	Locker Key Deposits and Record
	Chemistry Laboratory Locker Deposit
	Petty Cash Imprest Fund
	Loan of Equipment and/or Tools Deposit and Record Card
Recording and Activities	Recording of Activities Operations
	Permits Required to Withhold University Identification Cards as Collateral
Financial Reporting and Analysis	Inventory Record and Reports of Poultry Flocks and Produce
	Inventory Record and Reports of Meat Acquisitions, Usage and Disposals
	Central Animal Facility Accounting Procedures
Financial Policies	Directorate of Financial Services
	Proposals, Agreements, Contracts, Legal, and Other Documents

	Committing the University to Perform a Specific Work or Service
	Budget Surpluses and Deficits – Carryovers
	Transfer of Service Department Costs to User Departments, Programs and Projects
	Internal Financing – Loans
	Trust and Specific Purpose Funds
	Travel
	Hospitality Expenses
	Professional Development Reimbursement
	Establishment of Petty Cash Imprest Funds on Campus
	Donations in Kind – Appraisals, Receipts, Record
	Access to Donor Database Information University Affairs
	Collection of Students' Accounts Receivable
	Extension of Credit to Clients and Collection of General Accounts Receivable
	Commercial Credit Cards Issued in the University's Name
	Guaranteed Housing Loan to Faculty and Staff
	Relocation Expenses for Faculty Members and Professional Staff
	General Endowment Fund Management Policy
General Policies	Officers, Signing Officers, Signing Authorities, Execution of Documents
	Election Campaigning on Campus
	Management, Allocation and Leasing of University Owned Space
	Meeting Rooms and Lounge Space
	System Development at the University
	University Art Collection

	Soliciting of Donations and Administration of Bequests and Planned Giving Program
	Special Interest Group Fund Raising
	University Identification Card Plan
	Delegation of Authority for the Signing of Contracts
	On-Campus Advertising, Promotion, Sales, and Solicitations
	Special Grant Policy for Registered Student Groups
	Policy on the Privacy of Student Records
	Site License
	Conflict of Interest Policy
	Purchasing Services
	Campus Food and Refreshment Services
	Management and Administration of the Licensing, the Sale of Liquor, the Servicing, and the Areas for Consumption and the Possession of Liquor on University Premises
	Disposal of Surplus or Obsolete Furniture, Equipment or Materials
	Institutional Information Security
	Use of In-Line Skates, Roller Skates, and Skateboards
	Use of University Facilities Including Audio Visual Equipment
	Management and Use of War Memorial Hall
	Central Box Office
	Booking and Use of Livestock Pavilion and Stable Areas, paddocks and Pastures of Dairy Barn
	Room Reservations, Scheduling and Rental Rates of Hospitality Services' Controlled Space
	Delegation of Authority for Commitment of University Funds upon

	Budget Allocation
	Distribution of Graduate Calendars
	Distribution of Undergraduate Calendars
	Rabies Inoculations and Subsequent Title Evaluation
	Pets in University Buildings and Student Residences
Treasury Policies	Risk Management Policy
	Insurance Policy
	Waiver of Liability Requirement on Campus Workers of Non-Employee Status
	Accidental Damage to Departmental Equipment or Laboratory Supplies Caused by University Employees
	Investment Policy
	Borrowing Policy
University Affairs and Development Policies	Donations in Kind: Appraisals, Receipts, Record
	Soliciting of Donations, and Administration of Bequests and Planned Giving Program
	Special Interest Group Fund Raising
	Gift Acceptance Policy and Procedure
	Access to Donor Database Information University Affairs & Development Office

TOPIC:	**Hotel Management**
Functional Area:	**Hospitality**

Subject Area Category	Detailed Subject Areas
Accounting Manual	Introduction & General
	General Accounting Procedures
	Financial Reporting
	Payroll
	Regulatory Reports
	Night Audit
	Cashiering & Banking
	Chart of Accounts
	Glossary
Employee Handbook	Introduction
	General Work & Employment Conditions
	Your Pay
	Your Benefits
	Your Appearance
	Your Company Record
	Safety & Security
	Your Company Record (Repeat? Mentioned two cells above, as well)
	General Rules & Guidelines
	Guest Services
Guest Services Manual	Introduction & General
	Front Office Operations
	Reservations
	Guest Transportation
	Telephone Department
	Night Audit
	Front Office Management
	Reference
Human Resources Manual	Introduction & General Section
	Employee Recruitment Section
	Hiring Section
	Personnel Administration Section

http://www.marinmgmt.com/hotelmanuals.html

129

	Employment Insurance Section
	Training
	Separation of Employment
	Glossary
Sales Manual	Introduction & General
	Staffing
	Sales Management
	Sales Technique
	Competition
	Marketing
	Administration
	Event Sales & Service
	Reference
	Glossary
Safety, Security, & Emergency Procedures Manual	Introduction & General
	Employee Injury & Illness Prevention Program
	Guest/Visitor/General Safety & Security
	Key Control
	Emergency Procedures
	Security Department
	Reference

TOPIC:	**Information Technology Manual**
Functional Area:	**Information Technology (IT)**
http://www.doit.ca.gov/simm/default.asp	

Subject Area Category	Detailed Subject Areas
Risk Assessment Model	RAM Overview
	RAM Questions
	RAM Client
Management Memoranda	Internet Policy Management
	Project Management & Oversight
	Fundamental Decision Criteria for Approval of IT Projects
	Budget Change Proposal Review
	Project Initiation, Approval & Change Process
	Information Technology Oversight Policy
	Information Technology Acquisition Planning Policy
	Software Management Policy
	Information Technology Communication and Conservation Plan for Energy Management
	IT Project Related Communication
	State Agency Requirements Regarding Preventive Energy Management
	Energy Management Business Continuity Planning
	IT Project Submittal and Approval Policy
	IT Procurement Plan Technology Directive
	IT Project Approval Process Directive
	Process Control Exclusion for State Information Technology Projects
	Y2K Executive Order Exemption
	Clarification of Management Memo

Policies	Software Management Policy
	IT Project Submittal and Approval Policy
	Policy/Standards Development and Vetting Process Summary
	Policy/Standards Development and Vetting Process Diagram
	Statewide Internet Usage Policy
	Project Management
	Project Oversight Policy
	Feasibility Study Report Policy
	Project Change Request Policy
	Special Project Report Policy
Guidelines	Preliminary Feasibility Study Report (FSR) Guidelines
	FSR Guidelines
	Project Change Request Guidelines
	Special Project Report Guidelines
	FSR Reporting Exemption Request Guidelines
	IT Procurement Plan Template Guidelines
	Agency Information Strategy Documentation Requirements
	Software Management Guidelines
	Software Management Handbook
Checklists	Preliminary FSR Checklist
	FSR Checklist
	Project Change Request Checklist
	Special Project Report Checklist
Forms	Preliminary FSR Form
	FSR Form
	Special Project Report Form
	Project Change Request Form
	FSR Reporting Exemption Request Form
	Project Summary Package

TOPIC:	**Library Policies**
Functional Area:	**Any Library Management System**
http://www.sirin.lib.il.us/docs/cen/docs/lib/tablecont.htm	

Subject Area Category	Detailed Subject Areas
Mission Statement	
Statement of Objectives	
Library Bill of Rights	
Interpretations of the Library Bill of Rights	
Freedom to View Statement	
Freedom to Read Statement	
Policy on Confidentiality of Library Records	
Libraries Calendar Hours	
Internal Cash Controls	
Work Requests	
Sexual Harassment Policy	
Drug and Alcohol Free Policy	
Patron Behavior Policy	
Legal Basis for Material Selection Policy	
Computer and Internet Use Policy	
Policy Regarding Disposal of Surplus Library Materials	
Legal Basis for Policy Regarding Disposal of Surplus Library Materials	
Privacy of Circulation Records	
Photocopy Policy	
Disability Accommodation	
Fines	
Legal Basis for Overdue Fines	
Policy for Overdue Materials	
Lending Policy	
Gifts	
Holidays	
Hours	
Emergency Procedures	
Meeting Room	
Discovery Room – Learning Center Policy	

Internal Cash Controls	
Purchasing Policy	
Personnel, Staff Selection, and New Employees Policies	
Compensation	
Performance Evaluations and In-Service Training	
Staffing Changes	
Basis for Appointments, Promotions, and Salary Increases	
Staff Development	
Staff Relationships	
Bylaws of the Board of Trustees	

TOPIC:	**Medicare & Medicaid (HCFA) Manuals**
Functional Area:	**Health Care**

http://www.hcfa.gov/pubforms/htmltoc.htm	
Subject Area Category	**Detailed Subject Areas**
Coverage Issues Manual	
State Operations Manual	
Outpatient Physical Therapy/CORF Manual	
Hospital Manual	
Home Health Agency Manual	
Skilled Nursing Facility Manual	
Intermediary Manual	
Carrier Manual	
Provider Reimbursement Manual (PRM) Part 1	
PRRB Appeals Instructions	
Provider Reimbursement Manual	
Peer Review Organization Manual	
Hospice Manual	
Regional Office Manual	
State Buy-In Manual	
Carrier Quality Assurance Program Manual	
Medicare Rural Health Clinic Manual	
State Medicaid manual	
Medicare Health Maintenance Organization Manual	
Federally Qualified Health Maintenance Organization Manual	
ESRD Network Organization Manual	
Program Integrity Manual	
HCFA Business Partners Security Oversight Manual	
Medicare Managed Care Manual	

TOPIC:	**Nursing Manual**
Functional Area:	**Health Care**

http://www.health.state.mo.us/Publications/TBLEOFC.html

Subject Area Category	Detailed Subject Areas
Overview	Hospital and Clinical Programs Nursing
	Philosophy of Hospital and Clinical Programs Nursing
	History of Public Health Nursing
	Tenets of Public Health Nursing
Plan for Providing Nursing Care	Definition of Nursing Care
	Areas of Practice
Administrative and Organization of Hospital Nursing and Clinical Programs	Organization Charts
	Nursing Direction
	Medical Direction
	Committee Structure
Professional Practice Framework	Standards of Nursing Practice
	Standards of Professional Performance
	Code of Ethics
	Nursing Practice Act & Code of State Regulations
	Description of Nursing Titles
	Negligence and Malpractice
	Reporting Incompetent, Unethical, or Illegal Practices
	Delegation
	Collaborative Practice
	Case Management
	Home Visits
	Dispensing Medications
Utilization of Patient Care Areas	Admissions
	Transfers/Relocations
	Discharges/Transfer Out of Institution
	Closure of Inpatient Beds

Maintenance of Professional Practice System	Budget
	Delivery of Patient Care Methodology
	Patient Education
	Discharge Planning
	Documentation
	Nursing Standards
	General Nursing Policy Addressing Professional Behaviors
	Dress Code
	Attendance, Punctuality, Illness, and Reporting
	Special Disciplinary Measures
	Communications within Professional Nursing
Governing Rules of Professional Nursing Organization	General Safety/Risk Management
	Confidentiality
	Patient Support Services
	Legal Issues Within Department of Patient Care Services
	Medication Policies
	Visiting Regulations
	Volunteer Services
	Rususcitation/333 Code Policy for Nursing Personnel
	Patient Transport
Nursing Personnel Human Resources	Advertising/Posting
	Interviewing/Selection Practices
	Disciplinary Actions
	Orientation
	Preparation of Specification and Response Evaluation Criteria
	Performance Appraisal Practices
	Job Description Performance Appraisal Development

TOPIC:	**Patient Handbook**
Functional Area:	**Health Care (Hospitals)**

http://www.stpetes.org/healserv/handbook.htm

Subject Area Category	Detailed Subject Areas
Mission, Values, Vision, and History	
Your Hospital Team	Pastoral Services
	The Nursing Staff
	The Medical Staff
	Case Management
	Additional Services
Food Services	
Policies and Procedures	Visiting Hours
	Fire Drills
	Medications
	Oxygen
	Wheelchairs
	Valuable or Lost Items
	Electrical Items from Home
	Out-of-Town Visitors
	Visiting Regulations
	Gift Shop
	Condition Reports
	Waiting Areas
	Chapel
	Transportation
	Notary Services
	Gifts for Patients
	Health Information Library
	Mail
	Hospitality Cart
	Newspapers
	Flowers
	Patients with Disabilities
	Swing Beds
	Your Hospital Bill
	Health Insurance
	OB – Newborns

	Billing Policy
	Payment Options
	Financial Assistance Program
	Answering your Questions
	Personal Belongings
	Discharge Instructions

TOPIC:	**Personnel or Human Resources**
Functional Area:	**Any Industry**

http://www.howardcc.edu/hr/policies/table_of_contents.htm

Subject Area Category	Detailed Subject Areas
Employee Policy Manual	Purpose
	Policy Changes
	Confidentiality Agreement
	Personnel Administration
	Conflict of Interest Procedure
Equal Employee Opportunity	Non-Discrimination Policy
	Equal Employment Opportunity Policy
	Equal Educational Opportunity Policy
Affirmative Action	Affirmative Action Policy
	Affirmative Action Policy for the Employment of Minorities and Women
	Affirmative Action Policy for the Employment of Disabled Individuals
	Affirmative Action Policy for the Employment of Disabled and Vietnam-Era Veterans
Federal Laws and State Policies	Equal Employment Opportunity
	The Americans with Disabilities Act
	Family and Medical Leave Act
	HIV/AIDS Policy
Sexual Harassment	Sexual Harassment Policy
	Discrimination Compliance Procedures
	Diversity Procedure
Recruitment and Selection	Recruitment and Selection Policy
	Posting Announcements
	Recruitment of Faculty and Staff Procedure
	Work Eligibility Procedure
	Selection of Faculty and Staff Procedure
	Nepotism

	Hiring Process for Temporary Employees
	Hiring and Placement
	Testing Applicants for Employment
	Offer of Employment
	Procedures for New Employees
	Reimbursement of Travel Expenses for Employment Interviews and Relocation
	Transfer Policies
	Reinstatement of Former Employees
	Temporary or Regular Placement of Employees through Outside Agencies
	Affirmative Action Serious Search Policies and Procedures
	Criminal Record Check
Employment	Employment Policy
	Employment Definitions Procedure
	Probation Procedure
	Promotion (Faculty) Procedure
	Promotion (Staff) Procedure
	Resignation Procedure
	Retirement
	Layoff for Lack of Work or Funds
	Termination for Poor Performance or Failure to Comply with Policies
	Termination Procedures
Labor Relations	Unions Representing Service Staff
	Collective Bargaining
	Relations with Union Representatives
	Official Union Membership Elections
Employment Practices	Conditions of Work and Personal Conduct
	Responsibility of Supervisors
	Performance Review Guidelines
	Complaint and Grievance Procedures
	Policy on Conflict of Interest

	Employee Development Resources
	Relations with the Community and Public
	Policy on Workplace Violence
Compensation	Compensation Policy
	Supervisor's Responsibility in Payroll Matters
	Attendance Reports Procedure
	Overtime and Compensatory Time Procedure
	Expense Reimbursement Procedure
	Hours of Work/Payment of Wages Procedure
	Merit Pay (Faculty) Procedure
	Merit pay (Staff) Procedure
	Meritorious Service Award Procedure
	Outside Employment Procedure
	Salary Administration and Schedules
	Flexible Scheduling Procedure
	On-Call Status Procedure
	Shift Differential
	Making Up Time
	Special Holiday Closing
	Meal Pay
	Lunch Periods
	Break Periods
	Moonlighting
Performance Administration	Personnel Administration Policy
	Policy and Procedure Review Procedure
	Classification Procedure
	Job Descriptions Procedure
	Personnel Files Procedure
	References and Employment Verification Procedure
	Employee Recognition Procedure
	Status Change
	Name and Address Changes

Benefits	Benefits Policy
	Credit Union Procedure
	Direct Deposit Procedure
	Group Health Benefits Procedure
	Extension of Group Health Benefits Procedure
	Life Insurance Procedure
	Accidental Death and Dismemberment Insurance Procedure
	Short-Term and Long-Term Disability Insurance Procedure
	Restoration of Benefits Procedure
	Retirement of Benefits Procedure
	Savings Bonds Procedure
	Tuition/Fee Reimbursement Procedure
	Tuition Waiver Procedure
	Adjunct Faculty Tuition Reimbursement Procedure
	Federal Insurance Contribution Act (Social Security) Procedure
	Unemployment Assistance Program (EAP) Procedure
	Physical Fitness in the Athletic and Fitness Center Procedure
	Flexible Spending Accounts Procedure
	Adoption Policy
Employee Leave	Employee Leave Policy
	Administrative Leave Procedure
	Annual Leave Procedure
	Bereavement Leave Procedure
	Consulting Leave Procedure
	Holiday Leave Procedure
	Jury Duty/Court Appearance Procedure
	Leave for Religious Observances
	Leave Without Pay Procedure
	Liberal Leave Procedure
	Maternity Leave Provisions
	Military Leave Procedure

	Military Training Duty Leave
	National Guard and Civil Defense Call-Out
	Personal Leave Procedure
	Professional Leave Procedure
	Return from Leave
	Sabbatical Leave Procedure
	Sick and Disability Leave or Absence Procedure
	Time Off for Voting
	Family and Medical Leave Act (FMLA) Leave Procedure
	Emergency Leave Bank Procedure
Ethics and Conduct	Ethics and Conduct Policy
	Absence From Work Procedure
	Confidentiality Procedure
	Gifts and Honorariums Procedure
	Identification Cards Procedure
	Key/Access Cards Procedure
	Parking and Traffic Control Procedure
	Personal Mail Procedure
	Personal Telephone Calls Procedure
	Use of College Resources and Property Procedure
	Political Activities Procedure
	Proper Use of Information Technology Procedure
	Outside and/or Additional Employment Procedure
	Nepotism Procedure
	Employee Code of Conduct Procedure
	Events and Receptions Procedure
Employee Health and Safety	Employee Health and Safety Policy
	Sexual Assault Policy
	Communicable Diseases Procedure
	Emergencies Procedure
	Health and Safety of Employees Procedure

	Inclement Weather Procedure
	Law Enforcement Personnel on Campus Procedure
	Smoking Procedure
	Solicitations and Sales Procedure
	Unauthorized Persons on Campus Procedure
	Sexual Assault Procedure
	Fitness to Work Procedure
Drug-Free Campus	Drug-Free Campus Policy
	Alcohol Use Procedure
	Alcohol Abuse Procedure
	Drug Abuse Procedure
Suspension and Dismissal	Suspension and Dismissal Policy
	Dismissal of Tenured (Term of Contract) Faculty Procedure
	Dismissal of Tenured (Term of Contract) Staff Employees Procedure
	Dismissal of Tenured (Term of Contract) Employees Procedure
Office Rules	Dress Code
	Absence
	Ethics
	Gambling
	Drugs, Narcotics
	Insubordination
	Violence
	Injuries
	Fraud and Abuse
	Harassment

146

TOPIC:	**Project Management**
Functional Area:	**Information Technology (IT)**

http://www.doit.ca.gov/simm/ProjectManagement/ProjManagement.asp

Subject Area Category	Detailed Subject Areas
Project Management Overview	Introduction
	Concept
	What Is a Project?
	Roles and Responsibilities
Project Concept and Definitions	Introduction
	Project Statement
Project Management Planning	Introduction
	The Planning Process and Project Plan
	Activity Definition and Sequencing
	Development of a Project Schedule
	Budgeting
	Resource Planning
	Quality Planning
	Configuration Planning
	Top-Level Requirements Specification
	Risk Management Plan
	Project Plan Format
Project Start-Up	Introduction
	Baseline Plan
	Resource Commitment
	Starting Project Database
	Kick-Off Meeting
	Start-Up Checklist
Project Execution – PM Elements	Introduction
	Tracking & Monitoring Project Performance
	Project Reviewing
	Risk Monitoring Mitigation
	Change and Issue Management
	Corrective Actions
	Approval Process

Project Close-Out	Introduction
	Celebration of Success
	Post-Implementation Evaluation Report & Lessons Learned
Glossary	
Templates and Sample Forms	Project Management Plan Template
	Project Statement Form
	Project Estimate Summary Worksheet
	Risk Management Worksheet
	Project Start-Up Checklist Format
	Executive Status Report Form
	Status Report Form
	Change Management Form
	Issue Resolution Form

TOPIC:	**Purchasing and Business Services**
Functional Area:	**Any Industry**
	*http://www.asu.edu/aad/manuals/pur/*

Subject Area Category	Detailed Subject Areas
Introductory Material	Introduction
	Definitions
	Organization Chart
	Dollar Limits and Purchase Requirements
	Authority of the Purchasing Officers
	Delegation of Purchasing Authority
Ethical Considerations	Public Relations
	Code of Ethics
	Conflict of Interest
	Gifts and Gratuities
	Buying for Employees or Outside Entities
	Intent to Procure
	Public and Proprietary Information
	Anti-Kickback Guidelines
	Procurement Regulations and Authority - Procurement Regulations - Authority for Procurement - Value in Procurement
	Contract Signature Authority
	Prohibited Purchases
	Standardization of Common Use Items
	Procurement Process Overview
	Equipment with Support Requirements
	Records Retention
	Credit Cards and Store Accounts
	Establishment of Resale Activities
Orders and Requisitions	Order Transaction Types and Forms
	Purchasing Not Requiring a Purchase Order
	Internal Purchase Orders
	Quick Turnaround Forms

	Debit Cards
	Purchase Requests
	Traveling Requisition
	Tool Requisition
	Sole Source Procurement/Justification
	Cost Analysis
	Preparation of Specification and Response Evaluation Criteria
	Blanket Orders
	Departmental Limited Value Purchase Orders
	Reimbursements
	The Purchasing Card
	Bidding Requirements
	Emergency Orders
	Change Orders
	Retaining Consultants and Independent Contractors
	Competitive Sealed Bidding
	Competitive Sealed Proposals
	Procurement of Used Equipment
	Contracts for Supplies and Services
	Equipment Maintenance Agreements
Special Procurement	Special Goods - Live Animals - Hazardous Materials - Radioactive Materials - Books and Periodicals - Used Equipment - Foreign Purchases - Vehicles
	Special Services - Personal/Professional Services - Printing - Graphic Standards
Vendors	Vendor Information/Advertising - Information to Vendors - Advertising for Bids - Bid Security and Performance

	and Payment Bonds
	Vendor Selection - Purchasing Responsibility and Authority for Selection - Accepting or Rejecting Bids or Proposals - Aware of Contract for Goods and Services - State Contracts - Consortium Contracts - Equipment on Loan or Demonstration - Vendor Entry
	Small Business Program
	Contracts with Vendors
Price	Determining Price
	Competitive Bidding
	Installed Value
Inventory Management	Raw Materials
	Work-in-Process
	Finished Goods
	Consignment Inventory
Capital Equipment Purchases	Production vs. Capital Equipment
	Capital Expenditures
Receipts and Payment	Receipt - Reporting Receipt of Merchandise - Damaged, Short, Missing, or Duplicate Shipments - Return of Merchandise - Acceptance of Incoming Freight
	Payment - Lease vs. Buy Considerations - Trade-ins - Installment Purchases - Prepayment on Purchase

TOPIC:	Records Management (& Archives)
Functional Area:	Any Industry

http://osu.orst.edu/dept/archives/handbook/

Subject Area Category	Detailed Subject Areas
Records Management – General	Records Management Policies
	Records Management Justification
	Principles of Records Management - Records Life Cycle - Records Appraisal - Appraisal Considerations
	Records Retention and Disposition Schedules - General Records Schedules - Special Records Schedules - Retention Periods
	Filing Systems and Equipment - Filing Systems - Filing Equipment
	Reformatting - Microfilming - Digital Imaging
	Electronic Records - Legal Nature of Electronic Records - Formats - Electronic Records Retention Guidelines - Electronic Records Management Recommendations
	Confidentiality and Access
	Subpoenas and Other Court Orders
Records Management – Services to Other Departments	Personnel Files Maintenance and Access - Personnel Records System - Employment Records and Verification
	Temporary Inactive Records Storage - University Records Center - Departmental Centers

	Destruction of University Records - Disposing of Confidential Records - Disposing of Microfilms - Paper Shredders - Disposing of Non-Confidential Records - Disposing of Non-Record Materials
	Program and Function Change Assistance
	Disaster Preparedness, Response, and Recovery
Archives	Mission Statement and Access Policy
	Historical Holdings
	Transferring or Donating Materials to the Archives
	Reference and Duplication Services
	Exhibits and Outreach

TOPIC:	**Web Accessibility Standards**
Functional Area:	**Any Website**

http://www200.state.il.us/tech/technology/accessibility/iwas1_2.htm

Subject Area Category	Detailed Subject Areas
Purpose	
Scope	
Audience	
Relation to Existing Accessibility Standards	
Performance Criteria	
Implementation Guidelines	
Applicable Technologies	
Format of Guidelines	
Section	
Coding	
Text	
Colors	
Images	
Image Maps	
Audio	
Multimedia	
Animation	
Links	
Forms	
Data Tables	
Scripts	
Applets and Plug-ins	
Downloadable Documents	
Window Control	
Page Layout	
Page Content	
Alternate Accessible Versions	
Contact Information	
Testing	

Chapter 6

Epilogue

This book has provided the *best practices* for:

1. Developing policies and procedures that align to the vision, strategic plan, and core processes of an organization

2. Identifying core processes and deriving company manual titles

3. Drafting table of contents pages using table of contents examples and policy/procedure URLs

4. Benchmarking internal and external processes, policies, and procedures

5. Setting up a cross-functional team, selecting team members, and building an effective team

6. Using problem-solving techniques for defining a problem statement, diagramming the problem statement and identifying alternative solutions, choosing a single solution, refining the solution, and documenting the solution

7. Using a writing process and a standard writing format for writing policies and procedures

8. Using table of contents examples and policy/procedure URLs as sources of ideas, suggestions, policy and procedure examples, and "light bulb" moments

9. Using the Internet to search out content for table of contents pages and for specific policies and procedures

I have shared my successes with you, which represent the best of my 30 years of experience. Growth is a never-ending process. As your knowledge deepens about your organization's vision, strategic direction, core processes, and policies and procedures, so will your ability to build, develop, and write effective policies and procedures.

I have included my business address and contact information at the beginning of this book. Please let me know what perplexes you. Although I cannot guarantee flawless writing and success, I can assure you that you will be using the best practices when researching, developing, and writing policies and procedures.